# THE REALITY SHIFTING HANDBOOK

# THE **REALITY SHIFTING** HANDBOOK

A STEP-BY-STEP GUIDE TO
**CREATING YOUR DESIRED REALITY**
WITH **SCRIPTING TEMPLATES,
SHIFTING METHODS,
AND MORE ESSENTIAL TOOLS**

## MARI SEI

Published by:
Ulysses Press
PO Box 3440
Berkeley, CA 94703
www.ulyssespress.com

ISBN: 978-1-64604-318-7
Library of Congress Control Number: 2021946308

Printed in the United States by Kingery Printing Company
10  9  8  7  6  5  4  3  2  1

Acquisitions editor: Kierra Sondereker
Managing editor: Claire Chun
Editor: Kat St.Clair
Proofreader: Joyce Wu
Front cover design: David Hasting
Interior design: what!design @ whatweb.com
Production: Jake Flaherty, Yesenia Garcia-Lopez
Artwork: page 114 © BNP Design Studio/shutterstock.com;
    page 129 © Whale Design/shutterstock.com

# CONTENTS

# INTRODUCTION

Reality shifting is the transference of consciousness from one reality to another.

Here's a small anecdote: Imagine you're sitting at a table, dividing your attention between two cups placed in front of you. One is full of water, and the other is a strawberry milkshake. You make the decision to drink the strawberry milkshake—you reach your hand out, take the glass, and down the liquid before putting it back.

This action seems straightforward, a simple task. However, the concept of reality shifting is based on the premise that multiple reality shifts happened during that short story. For example, making the choice between the two beverages was a "shift"—your consciousness "shifted" to a new reality that was so similar to your previous reality that you failed to notice the shift in your waking life.

Unbeknownst to you, there also exists a reality where you chose the water. By making the decision between the two and eventually deciding on the milkshake, you shifted to a reality in which you have that milkshake. At the same time, the reality where you chose the water is ongoing, just like your current one. The reality you shifted to was determined by the simple choice between the two glasses. More shifts happened alongside this one, prompted by actions as small as the way you reached your hand out or the way your eyes moved during your decision.

This slight shift in reality is what we would refer to as a "minishift." However, when reality shifting is mentioned online and in practice, this is more often referring to a larger shift, after which our surroundings and ourselves are significantly different as compared to the shift in the anecdote above. This larger shift can be done while awake or asleep, using tools such as visualization, shifting methods, and meditation.

Both minishifts and larger shifts are a natural process of human consciousness. We often fail to detect the millions of minishifts we experience during our daily lives but would notice the difference a larger shift would make to our perception of reality. Most people do not experience larger shifts due to a lack of desire to experience one.

As a result of becoming widespread on social media, reality shifting has faced a string of misconceptions within the community. So much differing information

continuously being passed around has led to a frag-
mented definition of reality shifting that may vary from
person to person.

Some people have called reality shifting daydreaming,
or argue that people taking part in reality shifting simply have a complex and innovative imagination that
sways their perception on what life genuinely is.

Others, many of whom claim that you shift only while
you sleep, have deemed it lucid dreaming or other
similar concepts. Thinking this way provides easy
answers to a situation they've not yet been fully educated on. This means that many people have been
led to believe false facts about what shifting truly is.
As the discourse about shifting both permanently and
temporarily spreads online, they question longevity
(how long you can stay in your desired reality) and
verifiability.

These issues and misapprehensions are discussed in
greater detail in the upcoming chapters. As you learn
more about them, you will hopefully gain a firm grasp
on what is real and what is fake, which will help prepare
you for your own shift.

It's amazing that you're looking forward to beginning
your shifting journey! It's understandable that the
process seems a bit daunting and confusing at first,
especially since shifting is often seen as this massively
foreign and unfamiliar concept. It's something that
many of us have never even dreamed of before, so it's a

given that you may feel slightly intimidated or uncomfortable. This is natural! I was bombarded with these sorts of feelings too.

Back when I first got into shifting, it was a relatively new concept online and barely had a presence on community apps such as Amino and Reddit. While there were small communities of people supporting each other on their journey, it was hard to find beginner's guide on how to shift, and most members acted based on word of mouth or a few baseline shifting experiences from others. This is what inspired me to make my own community! Despite no longer being the owner of this community, it's amazing to see how it's taken off and grown over the years. A small Amino that had only 1,000 members skyrocketed to over 50,000 when the concept of shifting spread on social media. Now that it's taken off online, a lot more information is readily available by search for those interested.

A lot of information is compiled here in order to give new shifters the guide I wish I had years ago. This book consists of helpful tools and resources such as scripting templates, step-by-step shifting methods, and even more information on topics such as subliminals and meditation to give you enough insight to shift in a way that's tailored to your personal needs. Another aim is to clear up popular misconceptions (that I also struggled with at the start of my journey) and to clear people's minds of useless doubts and worries. See this book as your guide—pick and choose the topics you'd like to try out. By the time you're finished reading, not only will you have all the knowledge you need to shift, but you'll additionally be able to make or choose your own routine or method.

Happy shifting!

# CHAPTER 1

# WHAT IS SHIFTING?

The aim of this book is to try and keep all instructions clear and understandable for anybody first discovering shifting, not to be too overwhelming and confusing for the regular reader (trust me, I'm one of you). But to fully understand what shifting is, we'll first need to look into the scientific assumptions behind the theory of the many-worlds interpretation of reality, from which the concept of reality shifting arose.

The many-worlds interpretation was first proposed by physicist Hugh Everett in 1957, originally called the "Correlation Interpretation," and was later popularized by Bryce DeWitt and renamed to the term we use currently. To understand this interpretation of quantum mechanics, we first must establish that it assumes the realism of the universal wavefunction. Now I know this is beginning to sound confusing—but let me break it down for you.

Also coined by Everett, the universal wavefunction is "the fundamental entity" of the universe—all of physics is presumed to follow from this basic function. In simpler terms, Everett proposed that all systems of the universe can be compressed into one universal wave function. From here, after any given action, the universe splits to accommodate that action and give the subsequent outcome, similar to a tree branch model. Branches on trees begin in one larger formation and later multiply and split off in different directions as smaller branches.

When this concept was introduced, it offered an alternative to the Copenhagen interpretation. The Copenhagen interpretation is supported by the well-known Schrödinger's cat experiment, which I'm sure many have heard of.

During this experiment, a cat would be placed inside a box alongside four other things; a hammer, a container of cyanide, a container of radioactive material, and a Geiger counter, which detects radioactive particles. Assuming the correct radioactive material is used, there should roughly be a 50 percent chance that a radio-active particle would be emitted within an hour due to radioactive decay (a radioactive material getting rid of energy due to being unstable). If this happened, the Geiger counter would record a particle being emitted, and would then drop the hammer onto the cat, killing it.

According to the Copenhagen interpretation, we are unaware of whether that cat is alive or dead because we haven't yet peeked inside the box to check. Until the box is checked, the cat exists in two states: both dead and alive. There is no reality where the cat is one or the other. In a similar fashion, the Copenhagen interpretation states that particles exist in all of their possible states at once and can be influenced by the mere observation of an outsider, as shown by Schrödinger's cat.

While this could arguably be used as a basis for reality shifting, the concept shifters are more familiar with is the universal wavefunction interpretation. As explained earlier in the chapter, we shift based on a model similar to a tree branching out with each decision we make. Let's go back to the two choices of cups on a table, water and a strawberry milkshake. When you choose the water, you shift to the reality in which you have that desired outcome. This concept is supported by Everett's interpretation, in which the universe splits to accommodate actions, rather than multiple states existing all at once, as with the Copenhagen interpretation.

Now that we've established and defined what a universal wavefunction is, we can go back to explaining the many-worlds interpretation. This interpretation basically proposes that all possible outcomes of quantum measurements are realized in another universe. This implies that there are many more universes than we'd think, possibly even infinitely more, branching off in this tree-like structure. And this is the basis of reality shifting as we know it today.

That was the scientific summary, according to quantum mechanics, on what shifting is, but we should also define it in a much easier way to digest. To summarize, you can shift wherever you want. Whether you're shifting to be rich and famous, to your favorite book setting, or maybe to a similar reality where you're only making a few minor changes for your own happiness. These realities exist, and you can get there with the correct mindset and belief.

# WHAT TO EXPECT

When we think of shifting, it sort of seems like some far-fetched, sci-fi happening that feels like a completely foreign and fictional experience. I can assure you that it's not like that at all. However, despite shifting being a natural process that we've been experiencing throughout our entire lives when we make tiny movements and decisions, making a larger shift consciously does entail a few feelings and experiences we wouldn't get with mini-shifts. Additionally, it raises quite a few questions, which are about to be addressed in this chapter.

## 1. WILL THE REALITY FEEL AS REAL AS THIS ONE?

This is one of the first things I'd love to address, as it's a question almost every new shifter has at the beginning of their journey. The reality you're planning to shift to will be exactly like this one, only with the changes you're making. By that, I mean that it'll feel the same. Take your hand and touch the thing closest to you. Perhaps it's your bed or your phone. Touch it and really take in how it feels. Next, what can you smell? Maybe you can smell something cooking, or the smell of your freshly washed clothes. Maybe go and grab a drink or something to eat. You taste it, right? When you shift, none of this will change. Your senses will be exactly the same as this reality, and it will be just as real as this one. I've said this before, but we've been shifting since birth. We were simply unable to detect these shifts due to their minuscule and unconscious nature. These realities have always felt the same, right? They've always felt just as real, so why would that be different this time?

## 2. EVEN FICTIONAL REALITIES (SUCH AS FROM SHOWS, BOOKS, ETC.)?

A lot of realities taken from pieces of media are often called "fictional" realities, but these are actually not at all fictional. Are they fictional in this reality? Of course! However, if we're shifting to a reality where these people and things exist, they are no longer fictional and are instead real. Here's a good example: let's say you're shifting to meet your favorite character from your favorite movie. They don't exist here in your current reality as that character, but they do in another reality—in their reality where they are no longer from a piece of media.

# 3. WHAT DOES SHIFTING FEEL LIKE?

The answer to this question truly varies from person to person, and the way in which you shift can also have an impact on how it feels to shift. Different methods can give different outcomes, such as shifting while you're awake or asleep. Being asleep would mean you're likely unaware that you're shifting, and therefore you wouldn't feel or experience anything until you open your eyes and find yourself in your desired reality. If you're going to shift while you're awake through something like meditation, visualizations, or a method, you will be consciously aware of this shift.

The first thing I want to assure you of is that you won't feel any sort of pain or major discomfort. Apart from this, what the experience is like does vary from person to person. A lot of people report that they hear or feel things from their desired reality, or even see bright flashing lights while their eyes are closed, which I personally have experienced.

When I was shifting using my own shifting method, I was still as a statue, lying in bed. I felt that my arm was in a weird position, definitely not how I was actually lying. My arm was still in the same place physically, and I knew that, but it oddly felt sort of twisted. This wasn't a weird or scary feeling, and I continued my method until I suddenly began seeing colors spreading across my eyelids. I followed these colors until my body felt like it was spinning. Once again, I wasn't actually spinning—I was merely feeling a bit lightheaded as I was shifting—but it was a weird and new sensation to me. Last, I saw a bright, white light take over my vision. This bright light was unmissable, and actually gave me a lot of confidence in how real the shifting process actually is.

Those are some of the feelings I experienced, and a lot of shifters have similar ones. To further add to the sensations, people may also feel floaty, lightheaded, and could even feel their heart racing as they're shifting. This is absolutely nothing to worry about. Some people also shift with none of these feelings at all. Quite a few people have randomly woken up in their desired reality after just sleeping normally, so don't develop the negative mindset that you must feel these things in order to shift.

## 4. WILL EVERYTHING BE EXACTLY HOW I WANT IT?

Yes! When we script (which we'll go into more detail about later), or plan out our desired reality, our subconscious remembers every little detail. From things of major importance, such as your family or work life, to tiny things like smaller habits or your favorite TV show, nothing will be left out. You can trust yourself and your subconscious with the details.

## 5. HOW WILL I KNOW I'VE SHIFTED?

This part comes down to you and how you want to be made aware. Quite a few people script something that indicates they're in their desired reality, some examples being a specific smell or somebody waking them up. Some people even script that they immediately open their eyes after shifting, so as long as you have an intention to be made aware, there's no need to worry about knowing you're actually there.

If you haven't scripted any specifics, you can usually tell you've shifted through a change in atmosphere. Many shifters state that the atmosphere changes around them, and they know they're there. It's hard to picture this until you feel it personally, but if you feel like the atmosphere has changed or you've shifted, you probably have. The way the atmosphere changes will be different depending on what you've scripted. For example, your desired bedroom may be a little colder than your bedroom in this reality, or you may have scripted that you're waking up next to someone. If you feel this weight on your bed as planned, or perhaps feel a drop in temperature or notice a subtle noise you weren't aware of before, this is the change you're looking for.

## 6. DO I HAVE TO LIVE IN MY DESIRED REALITY FOREVER?

You can shift back to this reality whenever you want. We all have different reasons to shift; therefore, some people decide to stay in that reality for the rest of their lives. There's absolutely nothing harmful about this! Staying in the new reality permanently simply means that you don't have to shift back to this reality, and your consciousness will remain in your desired reality until (if ever) you decide to shift elsewhere. Still, if you don't want to stay there permanently, you won't. You can shift back in the same way you shifted there, or you can script a safe word or action to bring you back immediately on demand. For example, if you scripted that saying the word *cherry* three times in a row automatically shifts you back to this reality, it will!

## 7. WILL I DISAPPEAR FROM THIS REALITY WHEN I SHIFT?

Nobody will know you've shifted unless you want them to, and you certainly won't disappear. Your body here will continue as normal as there's still going to be a consciousness inhabiting it. When you've minishifted in the past, the person you were from previous realities hadn't disappeared. When you choose the strawberry milkshake over the water, and you shift to the reality where we have the strawberry milkshake, the you from the reality where you were undecided is still there, it's just that it's no longer your consciousness, but another, almost identical one.

## 8. BUT WON'T I FEEL OUT OF PLACE IN MY DESIRED REALITY?

Unless you decide to script otherwise, you'll have all the memories, experiences, and familiarity you'll need in order to feel comfortable when you shift. You don't even have to remember that you've shifted, and you could wake up as if you've been there your entire life.

# WHAT IS SCRIPTING?

Scripting is an optional process we use to set out and plan our desired reality in detail, making sure we have everything we want included everything we want without missing tiny, yet important pieces of information.

In order to understand, we can put "scripting" into literal terms. Imagine you're writing a movie script. First, you're setting it up and writing about your main character's physical features. You let their personality come out in your writing, and then you begin with the plot. Many different scenarios happen, and then you're finished. After that, your script is made into a film, and you can see your creation given life on the big screen. Scripting our desired reality is similar. We can script any past and future scenarios we'd like to happen in our desired realities before we shift and live these scenarios out.

Despite the comparison, scripts don't have to be set out in a script format. When people script, they often do it either in a document on their phone or laptop, or on paper. There's no set universal scripting template, and you can do it in any way that suits you and your personal needs. Personally, I like to set my scripts out in a mix of bullet points, subheadings, and paragraphs. I'll put my basic information (such as appearance, personal information, etc.) in bullet points, but then venture into more structured bodies of writing for information such as future scenarios or detailed descriptions of areas like my relationships to other people or my memories.

There's a range of other ways you can do this, which are explained in further detail in Chapter 5.

Not only can you script any actions you'll take in the future once you've shifted to your desired reality, but you can additionally script the actions of others. This is because you're shifting to a reality where every minuscule particle is set up to make these scenarios happen. You aren't controlling these people. If you didn't shift there, they would still have taken the same actions anyway as that reality exists without your influence, whether you script it or not. You're simply shifting to a reality where these things are already set up to happen and will happen.

When you're finished scripting, all that's left to do is shift! Scripting is, in my opinion, the most amusing part of the shifting journey, as it really makes me excited to finally shift and gives me motivation. Seeing your thoughts and feelings written out with the reassurance you'll be experiencing this in person within a matter of time is a euphoric feeling like no other.

But of course, scripting is definitely not for everyone. If you aren't interested in scripting, setting out your desired reality in your head is definitely enough to shift with. Scripting is purely to help with organization and is completely optional.

# WHAT ARE METHODS?

You've seen the word "method" thrown around quite a few times in this book already, and you're probably wondering what exactly the word means. Methods, in shifting terms, are routines or guides to help us shift. These come in all sorts of different shapes and forms, each one tailored to all sorts of different people in order to include anyone and everyone who wants to shift.

Methods are made by people in shifting communities, for anyone to use. The contents of these methods vary greatly, from visualization guides to entire shifting routines and guided meditations with audio instructions. Once again, these are not mandatory in order to shift. However, many find that methods have advantages that do help them shift. Some of these advantages may include raising your vibrations (which is not absolutely necessary, but can help you feel emotionally closer to your desired reality), improving your visualization and meditation skills, or simply motivating you to shift.

A lot of methods, especially since around 2018 when shifting began gaining a larger online presence, are visualization based. This means the method gives you instructions on what to picture in your head in order to shift. Some people can have trouble with these methods due to a lack of visualization ability, which is completely understandable! Each person has a different set of skills and abilities, and that's why there's now a range of method categories to choose from.

But visualization methods do have benefits. When we daydream, we often find ourselves feeling like it's actually happening, feeling the happiness or sadness that comes with the scenario we are imagining in our head at the time. This is visualization: truly feeling and experiencing the emotion that comes with imagining a scenario in our head. When we use visualization as a shifting method, we usually have our eyes closed instead of open, but this is the only conclusive difference. By visualizing our desired reality, we can feel like we're genuinely in it, which is exactly the point of these visualization methods. And by feeling the emotions that come with visualizing, our vibrations are being raised and our frequency further aligning with our desired reality, which will help us to finally shift. However, many have shifted while feeling down in the dumps, or without any effort or thought about shifting at all. Yes, raising your vibrations is a helpful tool that can come alongside visualization, but if you're struggling to do this, don't worry!

Not only are there visualization methods, but there are also methods with different themes and techniques! For those who can't visualize, *feeling* instead of *seeing* is often key to shifting. Feeling is such a vital aspect in shifting—meaning you should be able to truly feel the peace and euphoric vibration you would in your desired reality. Feeling once again aligns our frequency to our destination, and luckily doesn't always require visualization to get us there.

Some methods even involve falling asleep. A popular method in the community is shifting through lucid dreaming, which allows us to control our dreams as we sleep and shift by creating something similar to a portal inside the dream.

As previously stated, we don't need methods to shift. However, if you're planning to use one, they're often undertaken just before you sleep. Not all methods require a specific time of day to be performed, but a number of shifters believe trying to shift at night allows a more peaceful and quieter atmosphere, free from any sort of distraction or interruption you'd get in the daytime.

Now that you have a firm grasp on what shifting methods are, you can check out specific methods to help you shift in Chapter 8.

# CHAPTER 2

# COMMON MISCONCEPTIONS

The idea of reality shifting has arguably gained increasing attention within online communities since the early 2010s, with the popularization of subliminal messages and the law of attraction (the belief positive thoughts manifest positive results into your life), but the concept has been present for many years.

Subliminal messages (shortened to "subliminals") are often videos that, on the surface, look like they're simply songs playing over a thumbnail image. However, under this music hidden affirmations are playing at a much lower frequency, intended to reach the subconscious. These affirmations then can cause a positive change in a range of aspects in your life, from your mindset to even your physical appearance.

Subliminals then went on to gain quite a lot of attention on multiple different platforms. Some internet personalities lambasted the idea, yet large groups of people came together to establish communities dedicated to sharing similar interests in subjects entailing subliminals, manifestation, and the spiritual.

Many people interested in subliminals received results from the affirmations hidden inside the audios, which posed the question, why? Why are people getting results from a bit of text to speech behind some music? There has been lots of content explaining the science behind subliminals, describing how affirmations sneak past the conscious mind and leak into the subconscious to slowly begin altering our behavior. This is also further explained in more detail in Chapter 7, Subliminal Messages and the Subconscious Mind.

However, subliminals also opened up a gate to introduce the community to the concept of shifting. This started due to "shifting subliminals" making their first appearance. When subliminals were being used to aid in manifestation practices, such as laws of attraction and assumption, alongside changing people's lives and appearances, many debated the science behind the affirmations. While the explanation of the affirmations going straight to the subconscious is true and widely accepted, people began applying a multitude of theories and topics to the subject to bring something new to the community, birthing the widespread concept of shifting subliminals as we know them today. Shifting already had an online presence, but the introduction of subliminals to the concept made the process ten times easier for many, and definitely invited more people to research the topic further.

Shifting subliminals added a further explanation to the realities in which we do see results. Since shifting as a concept is mainly centered around the theory that there are infinite realities for each decision or movement we make, these shifts being so small we fail to consciously detect them, it made sense that this concept would be applied to subliminals and the physical/psychological changes subliminals bring upon us.

Those now interested in reality shifting believe that when we see results from a subliminal, such as growing a centimeter, we have shifted to the reality in which those results are true. For example, say you were listening to subliminals in which the affirmations would help you to grow a centimeter in height, and you do grow a centimeter. That's not simply a manifestation of your desire, you've actually shifted to a reality in which you're actually that height. This applies to any results gained from a subliminal. Shifting subliminals work in the same way, but they are intentionally tailored to suit reality shifting, rather than direct change such as hair color or height. Affirmations in shifting subliminals allow the user to consciously shift to the reality of their choosing. To summarize, we unconsciously shift each time we gain results from a subliminal. However, shifting subliminals let us intentionally and consciously shift to a scripted reality. These are mainly only used by shifters, not those simply looking for "normal" manifestation results similar to their current reality.

As shifting subliminals became more mainstream on video platforms, more people began joining online communities based around the subject of subliminals, affirmations, and manifestation out of curiosity, leading to the abundance of methods, experiences, and information we have today. What once started out as a smaller idea has now become a key concept in reality shifting and a means of happiness for those involved.

In 2020, shifting began growing even more due to its exposure on TikTok. Shifting had arguably been seen as an immature trend by a lot of users, and many misconceptions started to arise, with the definition of reality shifting gradually floating further and further away from its true meaning each time it was spread.

As a result of this, shifting is now not only seen as fake by a majority of people outside the community, but a lot of shifters additionally are fed false information and led to believe "facts" that may make their journey even harder. This chapter dives into these misconceptions, and clears them up through their true definitions.

# CLONES

The term *clone* is often defined as the consciousness left in this reality's body once your consciousness is transferred to another reality. But this is not an actual clone as many are led to believe. When shifting was first becoming popular, many wondered what would happen when you actually shift. Would people in this reality realize you had shifted? Would your body continue as normal? Would you act differently? Because people began asking so many questions, people who had experienced a shift came forward and explained this to us.

When we shift, there should be no difference to this reality at all. Nobody should realize you've shifted unless you decide to tell people. You should not act any differently to how you do currently, and nothing here will be damaged or jeopardized should you decide to shift back.

Clone sounds slightly reminiscent of science fiction, leading many to deem it foreign and strange. It insinuates that somebody else will pretty much be in your body, when in reality it's meant to be taken literally. A clone is defined as being "genetically identical" to its ancestor, which is exactly what the term means when used in a shifting. Your clone, left here in this reality, will be an exact replica of you. Your habits, speech and thought patterns will be exactly the same.

This is because your clone will still exist in this reality. If your clone were completely different to how you act currently (for example, if you try and script that your clone is a hundred times more intelligent than you), that would cause this to be a different reality. To put it bluntly, while you're in this exact reality, you have to remain like this. When you shift, your clone has to take your place currently—not the "you" in another reality where you're more intelligent, but the you that's here right now, as you're reading this. Clones are not some form of otherworldly stand-in for you while you shift: they ARE you, and there is no changing this fact.

A lot of people introduced to shifting in a more recent timeline have struggled to grasp this concept, as the definition of a clone is arguably one of the most misinterpreted and wrongly conveyed pieces of information in the entire community.

Online, specifically on TikTok, people made videos of their clones, apparently "after shifting." Some people would let their clones use their accounts while they were gone, and some videos displayed these clones acting completely differently from to the original account owner. This led to an abundance of comments poking fun at the clones, almost starting a trend of clones being seen as some sort of other—a completely different person with a different personality.

Though these were often widely believed at the time, these videos are fake. As stated previously, no clone will act differently from you in this reality. Your clone is *you*.

# THE LUCID DREAMING ARGUMENT

When we come face to face with a concept that may question what we've been taught for our entire lifespan, it's natural that we may try to rationalize it by applying it to a familiar concept. Since reality shifting spread online like wildfire, many people were understandably skeptical, especially due to the amount of misconceptions and false information developing around the subject.

Although shifting was an unnatural concept to most not already familiar with subliminals or similar topics, many had encountered lucid dreaming before. Therefore, people shifting on social media received an influx of comments saying that they were delusional, calling shifting "lucid dreaming" and even attempting to educate shifters on the topic.

As mentioned beforehand, it's understandable that people's minds may automatically lean toward lucid dreaming when hearing about reality shifting. Lucid dreaming is something more people are familiar with, and there are some similarities between the two. But to call reality shifting "lucid dreaming" is completely false. Shifting is in no way lucid dreaming. That said, there is a method of shifting that involves lucid dreaming, but this further reiterates that the two concepts are completely different. The fact that reality shifting and lucid dreaming are two different concepts is also supported by the different senses a person feels while participating in each.

During a lucid dream, we become aware that we're in a dream, and as a result we can then begin to control it and construct whatever we want in our mind. Many describe this as being a realistic experience, being full of joy and excitement while it happens. I remember my first lucid dream, which actually stemmed from a normal dream. I was at some sort of party in the garden of a house from my childhood with a bunch of my friends there. At some point, I was sitting next to a fire, and under this fire was a sandpit. I started drawing a heart in the sand—but as I was doing this, I realized my senses were starting to heighten. I could feel the sand underneath my fingers and could feel the heat of the fire, all the talking around me beginning to become too realistic to be a dream, I thought. However, our senses during lucid dreams are synthetic, meaning they're created by the mind and not actually being experienced by our waking body. Though the dream is realistic, the fact that the senses aren't a genuine experience often makes the dream feel not quite as real as we would like.

On the other hand, shifting feels as realistic and genuine as this reality, because it *is* real. Your senses will be there in another reality entirely, and everything you touch, smell, or taste will feel the same as it does here—or however you've scripted them to feel.

So, if all else fails, how do we tell the difference between lucid dreaming and reality shifting? We can do so through reality checks.

If you find yourself doubting that you're in a lucid dream, or perhaps you've shifted and are a bit doubtful that you have actually arrived in your desired reality, reality checks are an amazing way to give you knowledge on what around you is real and what is fabricated.

Though there are quite a few ways you can do reality checks, two of the most popular are the finger through the hand method and the holding your nose method. The first is where you put your hand in front of you, and you then try and put your finger through your palm. If your finger goes through your hand, or the physics of the scenario seem off, you can confirm that you are in fact lucid dreaming. The latter method involves your simply holding your nose and then attempting to breathe through it. If you can breathe, you're lucid dreaming. If you can't breathe, you can rest assured that you've genuinely shifted.

I recommend doing reality checks throughout the day, whenever you remember, in order to give them a bigger imprint in your subconscious mind. In my own experience, it's sometimes hard to remember to do a reality check when you're having a dream. When we do reality checks quite a few times during the day, we become more accustomed to it, and it will eventually begin to feel like a natural habit or process. Doing reality checks can also aid in our sleep. We frequently dream of things that have happened in the day, our mind loading knowledge and memories from our subconscious and replicating them during our sleep. If we continuously perform reality checks when we are awake, we have more of a chance of doing them in a dream naturally.

# ASLEEP OR AWAKE?

This misconception is another outcome of the forever-changing definition of shifting spreading on social media platforms. When reality shifting was first introduced, the definition was more universal—shifting your consciousness to one reality from another. As it got more popular, more people not previously educated on the topic took an interest, resulting in points being changed or altered to give the term a new definition. Personally, I like to think that there are two definitions for shifting; the correct original definition, and the definition born online that has now become widely accepted by the public.

This second definition treats shifting as something we do when we're asleep, which is also one of the reasons why many people, uneducated at the time when they heard about it, believed shifting to be lucid dreaming. Many online videos of people sharing their shifting experience consisted of the poster shifting during their sleep, and then being sad that they woke up in the morning and wanting to go back to their desired reality.

The misconception here is the part in which the person shifting wakes up, acting as if this is something that they can't help doing. Unless you script that you'd like to shift during your sleep only, and that you want to shift back when your body here wakes up, you will not shift back in the morning. Instead, your consciousness will continue in your desired reality while your clone continues your life in this reality, naturally. It seems to me that the people making these videos were lucid dreaming and not reality shifting, suggested by such terms as "waking up."

The reality is that you shouldn't wake up in the morning unless you were either dreaming or intended to do so. Shifting can be for any amount of time, whether that be only for a few days or permanently. You don't have to be asleep in order to shift, and you can consciously shift while being awake. But you can also shift during your sleep through simple intention or a sleep method such as the lucid dreaming method or the astral projection method. These methods are discussed more thoroughly in Chapter 6.

# PERMANENT SHIFTING

A topic many users online dispute is the correctness of shifting permanently and whether this is a morally justified route to take. When we shift permanently, this means we will stay in our desired reality without coming back to this one. The first thing I'd like to clear up is that permanent shifting is completely real and a choice you will have, yet many people do prefer to simply come back to this reality due to things such as prior commitments here or emotions towards their families, for example, keeping them here (which is completely understandable!).

However, deciding to shift permanently should not be something to debate in the first place. This is solely your choice, nobody else's. There are no consequences of not coming back to this reality. No, you won't shift back involuntarily and no, this will have absolutely no impact on your mental health or anything in this reality. Thinking this way is the result of putting your desired reality on a pedestal when really it's just as special and as normal as any other reality.

If you decide to shift back here after going to your desired reality, you're actually shifting to a different reality than the one you're in right at this very moment. We shift realities every second - every choice we make. No matter if you shift permanently or temporarily, you will not shift back to the exact reality you came from. Putting this into perspective, both permanent and temporary shifters will not go back to their 'original' reality, so why is this subject one for debate?

Overall, permanent shifting is in no way harmful or "wrong"; I for one will eventually shift permanently myself. This is your choice and yours alone.

# CHAPTER 3

# GETTING STARTED

Shifting seems daunting at first, right? You've been introduced to this otherworldly concept for the first time, perhaps through this book, or maybe you saw it online or through a friend and decided to do further research. Whichever way you stumbled upon the knowledge, there's no doubt that this is a lot of information to take in. Shifting is very fast and the internet is jam-packed with advice and opinions from other shifters. Reading through the contents of this book, you'll see there are a few chapters on different subjects such as scripting, meditation, visualization, and methods. To add fuel to the fire, there are some common doubts and worries that many people face when attempting to shift, but I address those and how to avoid them (despite their being a natural process) in Chapter 11. And, of course, there are the many misconceptions floating around the community that can be hard to tell apart from valid information.

I get that. I was in a very similar position when I first started thinking about shifting to my desired reality. I remember it clearly: I was sitting in one of my classes at the time, debating on whether or not to actually give it a try. Back then I was heavily into subliminals, and the night before, I'd actually stumbled upon a shifting subliminal. It really caught my interest and intrigued me, so I went on a tangent to try and find out more. Beforehand, I'd never even heard of shifting despite having been in the subliminal community for years at that time. I was guided to join a community app, which I'll mention and point you toward later in this chapter. As I joined that community, I was abruptly hit in the face with information that over a thousand members had posted.

There's a featured tab on this app, which makes it a lot easier to find the important, informative posts within the community. However, as a "baby shifter," if that's what you'd like to call it, having all of these posts readily available was extremely overwhelming. Suddenly, I had to think about what method I wanted to use. I had to consider my own strengths and weaknesses to figure out how to shift, I had to complete my scripts (which I hadn't even started, I might add) and even make a subliminal playlist solely based around shifting.

Luckily for me, the members of that community were incredibly kind, and I actually met one of my current best friends on there. I was given any help I needed, and I knew all I had to do for some judgment-free advice was make a quick post. Nevertheless, I'd hate for new shifters to be in the same position I and many others were in when first starting out. It's not worth the confusion.

As a result, this chapter is intended to be a simplified guide on how to get started on your shifting journey. Don't worry about any other chapters yet—none of them are important. All that matters right now is setting your mind straight and figuring out what you need to start shifting.

Think of this book like a sort of store. The main chapters are broad, detailing what shifting is and how to get started. The rest go into the finer details of different methods and actions you can take to further your journey. Now, let's compare this to buying a book or some supplies for work or your education. Let's say you're buying a book to write in and a pen. These are the basic tools you need to start writing. Similarly, these basic, broader chapters are giving you the tools you'll definitely need to perform your tasks correctly. But if you look in the store again, they also offer more items. There are some highlighters there, but you realize that they may smudge the pen and decide not to use any. However, you then see a ruler, and think that'll definitely be useful for the sort of work you'll be doing and decide to get one.

If you compare shopping to shifting, that's how I'd love this book to work for you. Just like the highlighters, not every single method or action will work for everyone.

Some people may not want to use a specific method, but may believe that simply listening to subliminals and meditating every once in a while is the best way to go. You don't have to get *all* the "supplies" from the store, only the ones that work for you.

After reading this chapter, maybe consider giving the more specific chapters a read in order to widen your knowledge and decide what's best for you. But, while reading this one, remember this is currently a simple process. Tidy your mind and get your bearings, because it's now time to prepare yourself and finally start your journey.

# WHERE TO SHIFT

Arguably, the most thrilling yet debatable part of your shifting journey is the very first part—deciding where to shift. This is something I still struggle with to this day, constantly changing where I'm thinking about shifting to and adding new desired realities to my list of realities I'd love to try out. Luckily for you, if you have this same problem, there's no limit to how many times you can shift! Don't worry about having a lot of ideas because right now, we're simply deciding on your first reality. Of course, this is assuming you aren't thinking about shifting permanently. If you are planning on shifting and staying in your desired reality permanently, this is the part where you'll really have to decide what you want and plan it all out! It's all extremely exciting!

First, it's important to note that all realities exist, and there's absolutely no limit to where you can go. That one TV show you really like? Go for it! So what if it involves superpowers? You're no longer in this reality, so *this* reality's rules don't apply there. A reality you've come up with entirely in your head? Not to discredit your creative efforts, but you haven't come up with that! That reality already exists and all you've done is chosen to shift there. The point is that all realities exist right now, and there are no restrictions on where you can shift to and live.

Now that that's in your head, we need to really consider which reality you'd like to go to.

## 1. DESIRED REALITY OR A WAITING ROOM?

Sometimes, it's hard to script when we have other commitments blocking the way. People often believe they're lazy or unmotivated to shift due to being too tired at night to actually script or even give a method a try, but this is actually often due to prior actions during the day taking a toll on your shifting routine. When I was a student, I often got home at around 5 or 6 p.m. after waking up at 6 a.m. to travel to school. My college was quite far away. When I got home, despite having a few hours of extra time, I only wanted to sit down and rest for a while, knowing I had to be up early the next day. In no way does being tired at night mean you're lazy, it just means that you simply don't have the time and energy to script or shift when you're back home or finished doing your tasks for the day.

A waiting room is a great way to get around this problem. A waiting room is a place where you shift in order to find the additional time and freedom you need that you might not be getting in this reality. More often than not, waiting rooms have simple scripting involved. Many people make their waiting room a bedroom or a nice house, somewhere they can relax in and be uninterrupted. It should be a place that you feel comfortable and at home in. Sometimes people also script a friend or an animal in their waiting room so they aren't too lonely. But overall, these waiting rooms—or small, simple realities—are used to help you script when scripting is too difficult to do in your current reality. These are incredibly helpful, because they don't take a long time to script due to their simple nature.

Because the purpose of waiting rooms is to script, people usually script their waiting room to have a notebook, computer, or something to write on so that they can finish their scripts in peace and quiet, away from the commitments of this reality. If you script a waiting room fast and shift there, you no longer have to worry about not having the drive to script and you can finally get it done with quite literally all the time in the world.

Back when I was in school, I decided to script a waiting room to give myself more time to shift without having to worry about the struggles of my daily life as a student. I first began looking at ideas on Pinterest and

Google, eventually finding a cute cottage I liked and basing my scripts around those pictures. I made sure I scripted everything I needed, such as a never-ending food source and somewhere to get toiletries, and I even scripted a cat to keep me company! To shift immediately, I scripted an app on my laptop that I was going to use to script. When pressed, a text box would appear saying "Shift to your desired reality?" If I pressed "OK," I'd shift immediately.

To summarize, waiting rooms are an amazing idea for those who may struggle to script in this reality. Once you're done scripting in your waiting room, you can then shift immediately back to this reality by scripting something in the room such as a button or an action that will immediately shift you, once you push the button or do the action. There's also no need to worry about waiting rooms just being an extra step in what can seem like a daunting or overwhelming process. Waiting rooms actually make shifting easier for those who simply don't have the time here in this reality.

If you're unsure whether you need a waiting room, I'd recommend trying to script your desired reality in this reality first to see if that's possible. If you're finding this to be too big of a challenge, you can easily script a waiting room, then script that your scripts from this reality are already in your waiting room. Then you can continue scripting your desired reality exactly from where you left off.

## 2. WHAT INTERESTS YOU?

If you want to go to a waiting room or straight to your desired reality from this reality, it's good to think about what actually interests you. Try to think of a reality that you're genuinely passionate about going to. If you're not passionate about your desired reality, your motivation to shift there will be hard to build up. It doesn't matter what you're most passionate about! Nobody will judge you based on where you're shifting to and it all depends on what you like the best. Try thinking of what you need the most, what your goal in life is, or what you're most into at the moment, such as a specific show or a celebrity.

## 3. WHAT WOULD LIVING THERE BE LIKE?

If you've decided on where to shift, you also need to consider what it'll be like when you actually shift there. Will this reality tire you out or put you in danger? This is more for the people shifting to an action-packed desired reality. If you think you're in danger of being severely hurt, stressed, or scared, it's a good idea to think about if you'll be able to handle these situations and the impact they may have on your mental health. But of course, there are ways to script that you'll be just fine in a reality like that. All your worries can be fixed by scripting, so you won't be in any actual danger if you script so. However, it's still good to consider this third point, just in case you change your mind.

# 4. DO YOU FEEL MOTIVATED TO SHIFT HERE?

Arguably the most important question to ask yourself: are you excited? Do you feel that anticipation and excitement in your stomach when you're scripting or visualizing? If not, you may find that you'll struggle to shift to your desired reality due to having little motivation or drive to do things such as methods or visualization in order to get there.

Does your reality interest you?

**Yes** — Would you be alright living here?

**No** — It's hard to build motivation to shift if your reality doesn't interest you. Perhaps think again and find one you like!

**No** — It's important you feel safe and welcomed. If you're unsure, maybe make sure to script things that make living there good for you.

**Yes** — Are you motivated to shift here?

**No** — If you aren't motivated to shift, you'll also find it hard to script. Maybe consider if this reality is really the one you want to shift to above others.

**Yes** — Is this the reality you want to shirt to most?

**No** / **Yes**

This is fine! If you aren't permanently shifting, you can shift to there later. If you are staying permanently, it's best to shift to the reality you like most.

# NEXT STEPS: SCRIPTING, METHODS, AND HELPFUL READS

Congratulations! You now know where you're about to shift and can move onto the next step—scripting. Scripting is the most exciting part, in my opinion, as you can finally see all your ideas come to life on paper or in a document (if your preferred scripting medium is online). We've already established what scripting is in the previous chapter, and a detailed explanation of all the scripting knowledge you could possibly need is coming up in Chapter 4.

After you've finished your scripts, you can begin to formulate a routine or a plan for how you'd like to shift. There are plenty of different ways you can do so—methods, meditation, subliminals, or a mix of these! These are explained in the next chapters, allowing you to pick and choose what's best for you in your shifting journey. It's important to remember that there's no wrong way to shift out of these methods, as long as you're comfortable.

Amino is home to the most popular shifting communities on the internet, and arguably the most useful place to go if you're looking for blogs about shifting experiences, methods, and advice. There are a range of communities you can join, such as Desired Reality Amino, Subliminal Users Amino, or Shifting! Amino. You can also find communities on other platforms such as Reddit, with r/shiftingrealities, and Instagram, under hashtags such as "dr," "shifting," and "desiredreality."

# CHAPTER 4

# SCRIPTING

So you've finally decided that you'd like to shift else-where, and you now know where exactly this place is. This feeling itself is pretty euphoric, simply knowing you'll soon be there and will be living somewhere that almost seems too good to be true. But what do you do now? You have so many plans and details in your head, and have no idea where to put them.

Scripting is an amazing way to get all your thoughts, plans, and ideas on paper (or if you'd prefer, a document online). You may already have your desired reality sorted out neatly in your head, which is completely fine! Scripting is a completely optional process that not everybody warms up to. Some people may find that scripting doesn't help them at all and just further untidies their shifting plans. But a lot of people find scripting to be extremely useful and efficient because they are able to see their desires set out in front of them. While you are visualizing, or if you want a recap before trying to shift or trying a method, looking over your script is an amazing way to raise your vibrations and give you a sense of familiarity and attachment to your desired reality. When scanning through, you may additionally find that you've left something out. It's easy to add to your script and, consequently, remember this new addition in the future.

# WAYS TO SCRIPT

As mentioned before, you can script in multiple ways. Many like to script in a traditional way—on paper. Writing things down is proven to increase your memory on the subject, and if they're able to write it out personally can give the writer a feeling of productivity or accomplishment, especially if they're able to physically hold their scripts. Another way to script is digitally. This could be on an application like Word, or maybe a notes app. Depending on your typing speed, scripting on a device is often a lot faster than writing it out by hand, and it's also a helpful way to insert any pictures or videos into your scripts without having to print them out. Despite this, scripting digitally does come with risks. You're able to lock the apps you script on through phone settings on most devices, which will stop curious eyes from scanning your scripts and save you any questioning. However, you'll need to be careful when backing up and saving your scripts. Having your scripts on your phone, for example, will also hold the lingering threat of lost documents; so ensure that your scripts are properly saved should your phone ever break.

Nevertheless, there's a quick and easy solution to the problems mentioned above, which is to print out your scripts. Having them printed means that you'll always have a physical copy in your hands should something ever go wrong, and that you will have most of the benefits of handwriting your scripts.

If you're someone who hates writing or planning stuff out, it may be best to keep your scripts in your head, unless they're too complex, and you feel getting them down on paper is better. If you're unsure about this, you could even define your own way of scripting. Possibly, if you're uncomfortable or too busy to write but don't want to leave it all in your head, you could create mood boards in sections of the script, with images or sentences that remind you of what you'd like to remember about your desired reality. For example, for the "appearance" section of your script, you could make a collage of pictures of your desired facial features, paired with short, snappy phrases such as "defined jawline" to go with this.

After weighing the pros and the cons, you can decide your preferred way to script, if at all. This information is a mere guideline, and you should decide which way is best for you based on your own work efficiency and how you like to get things done. The utmost important thing to remember is that scripting has no set rules. You can script to your liking, whether this is in extreme detail, or a few words or drawings jotted on a page.

# HOW TO SCRIPT

You've decided to script! That's a great first step, and the process from here is extremely exciting.

When I scripted my first desired reality several years ago, I found myself looking forward to scripting, which was remarkably out of character for a student struggling to even start essays for her coursework. I can promise you that the scripting process is awfully inspiring, and makes you increasingly happy thinking about where you'd like to shift. We've already gone through the ways to shift, so the "how to's" from here really do depend on your preferred method. This section's main purpose is to help you plan out what you'd like to experience in your desired reality, and how to properly format this to make it work in a way that's effective for you.

First, I'd like to establish some base reassurance and knowledge that the me from a few years ago would have genuinely benefited from hearing. The most important piece of information I can possibly emphasize is not to stress about fully remembering what you're getting down on paper. I know a lot of people, myself included, used to stress about our scripts, believing that if we didn't memorize every little word there, our desired reality wouldn't be exactly how we want it to be. While being able to remember your scripts is good as this can aid visualization, you don't have to memorize them in order to shift to your desired place. Our subconscious remembers all these tiny details, so as long as you generally know where you'd like to shift and you have the intention to go there, you'll be right where you want to be with absolutely nothing missing.

Second, don't begin to see scripting as a chore. We should script out of love and appreciation for the reality we'd like to go to, not solely because we "have to" script (which is false) in order to shift. It's completely understandable that you want to get your scripts done so you can finally begin practicing methods and shift, but there's nothing wrong with taking a break from it when you lack motivation or ideas. It's only natural that there will be parts of your script that are less exciting to write about, and sometimes this can impact your drive to get it finished. If you find this happening to you, simply take a break, move on, and come back later. When we start finding our scripts boring or troublesome, their quality severely declines due to less care being put into them. Much like a school project, rushing it will not give you the best result.

Now that those doubts and worries are out of the way, it's time to genuinely begin scripting.

One thing to lay out is if you'd work better with a template, or if you'd work better either forming your own template or just freely scripting in your own style. A way to work this out is by listing every possible category you'd like to script. For example, your basic information (such as name, age, and gender), appearance, where you live, your friends, family, and your job. This is a very rough summary of some things to script, and most people's scripts will involve way more categories than these simple ones. If you think you have a lot of information to process in your scripts, it may be best to either use or make a template to fully ensure you don't miss anything. However, if you're more comfortable with freely forming your own script and are confident you won't miss any important details, that's an amazing direction to take. If you're in need of some examples of a way to script or would like basic templates to use, there are a range of scripting templates that fit a variety of reality types in the following chapter.

Finally, the only thing left to do is write down everything you need to from your desired reality. As stated, there's no correct or incorrect way to do this, and it should be done in a way that works best with your personal preferences. Think of your scripts as your own canvas. Add pictures, drawings, detailed stories, anything! Whatever makes you comfortable or makes you visualize better is the perfect way to go. The purpose of your scripts is to get your thoughts on paper, not to conform to any sort of stencil or pattern. There's no wrong or right way to do it, and again, it's not essential in order to shift.

Once your scripts are finished, you can then shift! Of course, your scripts don't have to be completely finished, as long as you know what you want. But finishing your scripts may be seen as a form of completion. A lot of people decide to finish beforehand for peace and clarity of mind. Once again, this part is completely up to you. Don't think of your scripts as work that needs to be finished, but as an optional aid to your shifting journey that progresses at your own pace.

# SCRIPTING MISCONCEPTIONS

As with various other shifting topics, scripting also comes with quite a few doubts and misconceptions that need clearing up to ensure misinformation comes to a stop. A lot of information spreading around about scripting comes from subliminal affirmations and the way they're written. These affirmation "rules" later spread to scripting, when in reality the two sets of writing are completely different.

An example of this is the false belief that you can't use negative words in your scripts. This particular stance stemmed from subliminal affirmation formatting, as a lot of subliminal makers in the past lambasted the use of words such as *no* and *don't* due to their so-called effects on the subconscious. Many believed negative affirmations would have a similar effect on the subconscious, with the mind picking up on only the negative words and acting on them. This is false, especially for scripting. Your scripts are simply a device to aid your shifting journey, and negative words will have no impact on this. You can craft your sentences in absolutely any way possible, and your scripts will still work perfectly.

Many also are led to the opinion that scripts should be extremely detailed and precise in order to perfect the reality you're shifting to. This is, again, inaccurate. No matter which way you format your scripts, they're all just as useful. A script consisting of images and a few short sentences is no less powerful than a novel-length script going into utmost detail about each facial feature.

One of the most misinterpreted topics is scripting relationships in your desired reality. A lot of people have the idea that by scripting a relationship or love interest, you're then forcing that person to be with you or have feelings for you. I'd like to restate that when you shift, you're not making a reality from scratch. Even without your influence, life in this reality would still go on according to your scripts whether you shift there or not. This is because your scripts are already set out to happen. We're shifting to a preexisting reality, and your scripts are choosing which reality to go to, not creating it. This person still has feelings for your desired self even if you haven't shifted there, so scripting any sort of relationship is not at all harmful! You're not forcing them into anything and you're merely shifting to a reality where this was always going to happen.

# CHAPTER 5

# SCRIPTING TEMPLATES

When scripting, it's extremely easy to leave out certain details that are important to include in your scripts, or to simply think about if you've decided not to script. We often don't even consider pieces of information that may seem minuscule but can actually play a big part in making our desired reality perfectly tailored to us and our needs. A way to combat this is through the use of scripting templates. Scripting templates give you a set list of categories to include in your shifting journey, ensuring that no details or particulars are missing.

Of course, each person's desired reality is different, which also means that scripting templates will not fully fit the reality you're planning to shift to. However, this chapter offers a range of templates you can mold and change to your liking in order to fit your own preferences. The way you use these templates is up to you! These are simply a guide.

# BASIC SELF TEMPLATE

This is a template detailing all information about yourself, from major characteristics like your personality, appearance, and detailed relationships with your family members, to small things like your shoe size. Due to its basic and straightforward nature, this template should be applicable to just about any desired reality you can think of! This template split into sections to make it easy to scan and find the parts you may need.

## SECTION 1: BASIC DETAILS

This first section is your basic information such as name, age, and where you live. Think of it as filling out a form about yourself, but from your desired self's point of view.

Name:

Nicknames (if you have any—these could be names your friends or family like to call you):

Title/s:

Age:                    Date of birth:

Star sign:

Place of birth:

History (*this may include places you've lived in the past*):

_____

_____

_____

_____

Sex:                 Gender:

Pronouns:

Sexuality:

Nationality:

Race:

Ethnicity:

Species (*if applicable*):

# SECTION 2: APPEARANCE

Here you should fill out all information about how you look. This ranges from your face shape to your body type, to even the way in which you think or want people to perceive and judge you, based on the appearance of your desired self.

For some of these first categories describing your skin, eyes, lips, and hair, you could also use a picture or reference photo if that helps you get a better visualization of your desired self.

Skin description:

Skin color:

Eye description:

Eye color:

Lip description:

Lip color:

Hair description:

Hair color:

Special features *(such as freckles, birthmarks on your face, etc.)*:

Face claim *(This part is for if you'd like to look like someone else in your desired reality, a celebrity for example. If you're scripting digitally, perhaps insert a picture of them here. If not, just write their name and maybe a few of their specific facial descriptions you're aiming for.)*:

Weight:                    Height:

Specific body measurements *(insert any specifics, such as waist size, bust size, or hand length)*:

_____

_____

Shoe size:
_____

Clothing sizes:
_____

Special features:
_____

Body claim *(This part is for if you'd like to look like someone else in your desired reality, a celebrity for example. If you're scripting digitally, perhaps insert a picture of their body here. If not, just write their name, and maybe a few of their specific body descriptions you're aiming for.)*:

_____

_____

_____

When people see you for the first time, what do they think? *(This is like a first impression. Perhaps you want to be seen as conventionally attractive. Or a successful CEO. If you have any specific traits relative to your desired reality, this might have an impact on how people see you, and you may want to add that here.)*

_____

_____

_____

Additional information: *(For this part, you may want to add some extra information about how others perceive you. For example, you may have a natural smell. Perhaps you want to add a quirk like having no body hair or having eyes that change colors. The possibilities are endless.):*

_____

_____

_____

## SECTION 3: PERSONALITY

This section is to fill in any changes you may have to your personality or how you act! It's also good to add any talents here.

Personality *(How do you act? Maybe you're scripting an entirely new personality, or just changing certain things like being kinder, being more confident, etc.):*

_____

_____

_____

When people meet you for the first time, what do they think? *(Unlike the other section, this is what they think of your personality and how you act based on first impressions. Do they take an immediate liking to you?)*

---

---

---

Talents: *Add any talent claims or similar here (for example, "I have _____'s dancing skills).*

Likes:

Dislikes:

Hobbies:

How you act in any specific circumstances *(An example of this is how you act when you're embarrassed or when you're excited. Not everyone may want to fill this section, as it's quite precise.):*

---

---

---

## SECTION 4: RELATIONSHIPS

For this section, you'll have to choose what to fill in to make it applicable to your family/friends. I've included quite a few family members here, but there's also a broad template at the bottom of the list!

# FAMILY

**Parent's name:**

Basic information (age, birthday, etc.):

Appearance:

Personality:

What's your relationship like?

Your past with this person:

_____

_____

_____

_____

**Parent's name:**

_____

Basic information (age, birthday, etc.):

_____

Appearance:

_____

_____

Personality:

_____

_____

_____

_____

What's your relationship like?

Your past with this person:

**Sibling's name:**

Basic information (age, birthday, etc.):

Appearance:

Personality:

What's your relationship like?

Your past with this person:

**Sibling's name:**

Basic information (age, birthday, etc.):

Appearance:

_____

_____

_____

Personality:

_____

_____

_____

_____

What's your relationship like?

_____

_____

_____

_____

Your past with this person:

_____

_____

_____

_____

## Family member's name:

What are they (aunt, uncle, etc.)?

Basic information (age, birthday, etc.):

Appearance:

Personality:

What's your relationship like?

Your past with this person:

_____

_____

_____

_____

Additional information:

_____

_____

_____

_____

**Family member's name:**

_____

What are they (aunt, uncle, etc.)?

_____

Basic information (age, birthday, etc.):

_____

Appearance:

_____

_____

Personality:

_____

_____

_____

What's your relationship like?

_____

_____

_____

Your past with this person:

_____

_____

_____

Additional information:

_____

_____

_____

_____

# FRIENDS

**Friend's name:**

Basic information (age, birthday, etc.):

Appearance:

Personality:

What's your relationship like?

Your past with this person:

_____

_____

_____

_____

Additional information:

_____

_____

_____

_____

**Friend's name:**

_____

Basic information (age, birthday, etc.):

_____

Appearance:

_____

_____

Personality:

_____

_____

_____

_____

What's your relationship like?

_____

_____

_____

_____

Your past with this person:

_____

_____

_____

_____

Additional information:

_____

_____

_____

_____

**Friend's name:**

Basic information (age, birthday, etc.):

Appearance:

Personality:

What's your relationship like?

Your past with this person:

_____

_____

_____

_____

Additional information:

_____

_____

_____

_____

## SIGNIFICANT OTHER(S)

**Partner's name:**

_____

Basic information (age, birthday, etc.):

_____

Appearance:

_____

_____

Personality:

What's your relationship like?

Your past with this person:

Additional information:

## PETS

**Pet's name:**

Basic information (age, birthday, etc.):

Appearance:

Personality:

What's your relationship like?

Your past with this animal:

Additional information:

_____

_____

_____

_____

_____

# SECTION 5: LIVING SPACE

Here, you can write all about where you live, whether that's alone, with friends or still with your family. You can also describe exactly what your home looks like, in as much detail as you want.

Address:

_____

_____

Town/City:

Country:

Living with:

_____

Exterior:

_____

_____

Interior (where applicable):

Entry:

Living room:

Kitchen:

Dining room:

Bathroom(s):

Bedroom(s):

Hallway(s):

Attic:

_____

_____

Garden:

_____

_____

_____

_____

Additional information:

_____

_____

_____

_____

# WAITING ROOM
# TEMPLATE

This template is for those of you that think a waiting room will be beneficial to your shifting journey! This script is shorter than others and will help you plan out a basic room or world to live in temporarily while scripting.

Where is the waiting room? (*Is it in a country in this reality? Maybe it's underwater or somewhere that doesn't exist here!*)

_____

_____

Is anybody there with you?

Exterior:

Interior:

Personal belongings:

*(Anything you own in your waiting room! I'd recommend adding something to script with and keep you busy.)*

## ADDITIONAL PROMPTS

How will you shift when you're done scripting? *(Using a button perhaps? Or maybe a word you can say to shift immediately?)*

How is your health while you're there? *(Not getting sick, no periods, etc.)*

Where are you getting food and other necessities from?

# SOCIAL MEDIA TEMPLATE

**Platform:**

Username/Display name:

Content *(streams, art, music?)*:

Amount of followers:

Average amount of likes/viewers per post:

What kind of people watch your content?

What are your followers like?

_____

_____

_____

How do they interpret or see your content?

_____

_____

_____

Additional information:

_____

_____

_____

## Platform:

Username/display name:

_____

Content *(streams, art, music?)*:

_____

Amount of followers:

_____

Average amount of likes/viewers per post:

What kind of people watch your content?

What are your followers like?

How do they interpret or see your content?

Additional information:

# FAME TEMPLATE

Occupation:

How did you get into this occupation?

Are you under a company/agency?

How are you treated here?

Do you work solo or with others in a group?

When did your career start taking off?

What's your fanbase like?

Do you take part in any activities outside your job?

_(TV interviews, modeling on the side, etc.)_

Additional information:

_(This is where you can script any smaller details. Some things to think about are if you want to get into any scandals, or maybe you'd like to script that your fans respect your boundaries and don't invade your privacy! If you're a singer, for example, this could be where you script your albums or songs.)_

# SCENARIO TEMPLATES

These templates are for when you'd like a specific event to happen after you've shifted. What this event could be depends on your desired reality, but a few examples include a fight between you and a villain, a first date with the person you love, or meeting somebody for the first time.

**Scenario name:**

Date:

People involved:

Any context surrounding the event:

What happens?

**Scenario name:**

Date:

People involved:

Any context surrounding the event:

What happens?

**Scenario name:**

Date:

People involved:

Any context surrounding the event:

_____

_____

_____

_____

What happens?

_____

_____

_____

_____

# CHAPTER 6

# VISUALIZATION AND MEDITATION

When it comes to methods or any sort of shifting practices, you may find that they include steps for other actions, such as visualization, or some tips taken from meditation techniques. Both of these are incredibly helpful in aiding your shift, pushing you that one step further and helping you obtain maximum concentration and potential when trying or preparing to shift.

Though these may seem like added steps, it's once again important to note that many methods use visualization and meditation, instead of their just being stand-alone practices. For example, the elevator method (detailed in Chapter 8) uses both visualizations and breathing techniques used in meditation to make the method work. Also, in Chapter 7, you can see that there are countless videos and audio guides on YouTube offering listeners guided meditations to run them through methods, start to finish. Visualizing or meditating outside of a method can also be extremely beneficial to your shifting journey, and even in your everyday life in this reality!

In this chapter, we'll be looking into what meditation and visualizations truly are and the effects they have on your mind in order to elevate the shifting process. By the end of this chapter, you'll be able to use both of these in your shifting routine, assuming you find that they are helpful to you.

# VISUALIZATION

Visualization is a technique used to and live out our desires inside our brains so that they manifest in real life. It is something we've been practicing for our entire lives, and I can promise you that you're a million times better at it than you think. To begin this section, here's a small exercise to take part in and test out your visualization skills.

Let's imagine something that would make just about anybody reading this euphoric—winning the lottery. While reading these upcoming paragraphs, visualize this scenario inside your head and really try to pull these emotions to the surface.

You're exhausted, just getting back home after a long day. As you walk in, the comforting smell of *home* takes over your senses. Finally. You take your bag off and throw it to the floor, but as you do so, a small piece of paper slips its way out onto the carpet. It's the lottery ticket, you remember. Having been busy the last few days, you forgot to check the results after buying it. You debate checking the ticket for a while because it's so late at night. All you want to do at this moment is change clothes and get straight into bed. However, the tiny inkling of curiosity inside your body urges you to check the ticket before doing so.

You bend down and grab the ticket. As it slots between your fingers, you feel the smooth, delicate paper graze your skin. Straight away, you grab your phone out of your pocket and your hand is met by the cold glass back of it. You swipe your thumb across the screen to input your password and navigate your way to the internet.

The lottery numbers are now in front of your eyes, and you check each number one by one. You check the first number on your ticket, scanning the dimly lit smartphone for a match. After laying your eyes upon it, your stomach begins building up with the slightest bit of anticipation for the next one. Second one, you think. Upon seeing another one of your numbers, this pit in your body gets stronger and stronger. This feeling increases as next comes the third, fourth, and fifth, and you're finally left with the final bonus number. Heat is rising from your stomach to the rest of your body, but it's too early to get this excited. Your eyes dart across the page, and the eagerness in your stomach almost feels like it's about to explode at the sight of the number you're looking for.

You won! You drop your phone, hearing it fall with a thud and seeing it rattle from side to side a bit before resting on the ground. Your hands slap your mouth, gasping in disbelief. A smile paints your face when you bend down once again to grab your phone and tell your family about the event, but you hesitate as one question pops into your mind. What will you do with the money? Maybe you want to buy a house or give a lot to charity. Think about what you're going to do with the millions you've won.

That's the end of the exercise!

What you just did was visualize winning the lottery. If you did this correctly, you should've felt the pure happiness and feelings of anticipation when reading the numbers and realizing you won. Additionally, notice how most of the five senses were incorporated, which were intended to make you feel like you were truly experiencing them yourself. The ending question on what you'd do with the money was added to make you consider your options, not as the you reading this book right now (unfortunately), but as the person in the visualization who just won the money.

This is, in essence, exactly what visualization is. Visualization is when we imagine something in our heads, similar to when we daydream. By coming up with an image or scenario, truly feeling the emotions in those scenarios and using our senses to act as if we're genuinely there in person, our vibrations become raised, and our frequency becomes more aligned with that of our desired reality. This is arguably one of the most common and helpful components in countless methods and meditations used for shifting. While it's possible to shift solely through visualizing something realistically enough, methods will often ask you to do something more on top of visualization.

Visualization doesn't just have to be paired with other methods. Visualization is actually a great way to bring your scripts to life and aid your shifting journey whenever you find yourself having a bit of spare time. Often done as a part of a routine, you can do it at any time of the day to bring you closer to your desired reality.

Now you may be wondering... "So, what do I do?" Below is a step-by-step guide on effective visualization! You don't absolutely have to follow these steps, but for those unsure on how to start visualization, this should hopefully bring a bit of comfort and make the process easier.

# 1. PICK OUT A PART OF YOUR SCRIPTS.

The first step is to take out a part of your scripts to visualize. Some people may have scenarios scripted that will take place in the future or are a part of their past, and these can be great to practice your visualization skills. But if you don't, it's fine to simply visualize something like your appearance from someone else's point of view. Another option is to run through what you think your typical day will be like in your desired reality!

## 2. FIND THE PERFECT VISUALIZATION ENVIRONMENT.

This step is very subjective depending on what you find relaxing or motivational. For example, I love to visualize to music that matches the feeling of the scenario playing out in my head. Any sort of happy environment is matched with upbeat, pop-style music. On the other hand, a lot of people may find that a quiet setting is what works best for them in order to put their full undivided focus on what's playing out in front of them. Either way, find a place that works for you.

## 3. SIT BACK AND LET IT PLAY OUT.

Run through the visualization scenario in your head. There's no time limit on this! Restart it as many times as you need, replay the good parts and make sure you're having fun while doing it. Think of it as if you're watching a movie in your head, but also remember this is *you* in the visualization. You'll be living this out soon. Amazing, right?

## 4. REMEMBER TO FEEL.

This is the most important step by far, as this is what raises your vibrations to match the frequency of your desired reality. You have to try to feel what's going on in your head, no matter if it's heartbreaking, action-packed, or romantic. Not only should you replicate emotions, but you should additionally visualize the five senses. What can you see, hear, taste, touch, or smell?

Perhaps make a point of running your fingers across the wall while walking, or savor the feeling of holding somebody's hand, if your visualization includes that scenario

These steps can be used as often as you want! Visualization is something you can take part in at any time of the day. I personally love to visualize before I fall asleep, or if I find any time when I'm making a long journey somewhere during the day. By visualizing, you'll facilitate your shifting journey even more.

# MEDITATION

Unlike visualization, meditation is most likely a new concept for many people. You may have heard of it, but how many of you have actually tried to meditate? I also never tried it until I decided I wanted to shift. But after trying meditation for the first time, I realized that I never even stumbled across posts about meditation in the first place. In this section, we'll be focusing on how meditation can push you to shift. However, you'll also learn that it can be a useful tool in your daily life, shifting or not.

Meditation is to the brain what exercise is to the other parts of our body, and often involves training our mind to stay focused without wandering off its natural thought process. When we meditate, we teach our mind to maintain focus instead of thinking about other topics. When the mind wanders elsewhere, we quickly bring our attention back to something such as our breathing or the feeling of our body, and we empty our head once more. By doing this repeatedly, you will begin to see an increase in focus and mindfulness, alongside increased calmness and empathy.

There are a range of different ways to meditate, but a few include methods such as progressive relaxation and breath awareness to build focus on one thing.

Progressive relaxation is the practice of relaxing your body limb by limb, most often used to help with relaxation and sleep. This can be done in a range of ways, but arguably the most popular is tensing your muscles one by one. Start from your toes. Tense them, move them upward, downward, and then fully relax. Once this is done, begin tensing your calf muscles and work your way up your entire body in sections. You should also tense your facial muscles, such as your eyebrows and mouth. Once you've completed this, your body should be in an extremely relaxed state.

The aim of breath awareness is to focus on your breathing, and *only* on your breathing. You can begin by lying down and relaxing your body. Take a few minutes to completely relax and feel at ease, then shift your attention to your breathing pattern. You can let yourself breathe naturally and follow the default pattern you're breathing at, or you can set yourself a "routine" of sorts: breathe in for three seconds and out for three seconds, for example. Just let your mind maintain its focus. You may find your mind going off topic from time to time, so simply bring your full attention back to your breathing as a response. You can do this for as long as you'd like, but doing it every so often can increase your focus. Not only does this aid in shifting, but also in your everyday life.

Clearly, meditation is something amazing to implement in your normal day-to-day routine to increase the effectiveness of your own mind. However, how does this make shifting easier for a lot of people?

As mentioned previously, meditation allows us to maintain our focus on one particular thing instead of other thoughts. At the moment, we're sadly still in this reality. Visualization is great to raise your vibration, but it's hard to ignore the world progressing around you while you're watching your desired reality scenario unfold in your head. Imagine visualizing after or during meditation—pairing the benefits of meditation with the benefits of visualization. Doing both of these together is the recipe for a perfect shifting routine. Even without visualization, meditation still serves as a helpful aid to your shifting journey as there are countless guided meditations online specifically tailored to help you shift.

# CHAPTER 7

# SUBLIMINAL MESSAGES AND THE SUBCONSCIOUS MIND

The mind is an exceptionally complex maze of memories, with the subconscious clinging onto things we can't bring to our conscious mind voluntarily. While the conscious holds onto the present, ruling over our thoughts in the current moment and acting similarly to a short-term log, the subconscious mind is like a memory bank, filled to the brim with things both small and big that we've encountered throughout our lives. Subconscious material can range from faces of people we've passed on the street to past feelings and experiences. Due to the intricate nature of the mind, many people have utilized the subconscious to change their present via a process known as subliminal messaging.

# WHAT ARE SUBLIMINALS?

Subliminals are videos or audios that sound like music, yet have a deeper underlying meaning because they contain hidden affirmations that are meant to be undetectable to the listener's conscious mind. The audio of a subliminal has multiple layers, the loudest one being some form of music to occupy the conscious mind. At the same time, hushed affirmations are layered under the music, often playing multiple times to gain the attention of the subconscious.

As mentioned, our conscious mind struggles to bring information from the subconscious to the surface unless prompted to do so. These affirmations are extremely hard to consciously pick up on unless the subliminal is played at a higher frequency. Therefore, the affirmations go straight to the subconscious. Additionally, auditory subliminal messages are frequently played at such a high speed that sentences are rendered incomprehensible to the consciousness, further facilitating the power of the subconscious to absorb the hidden affirmations behind the music.

The information bypassing the conscious mind plays a large role in the effectiveness of subliminals. While your consciousness may put up barriers when being influenced by certain messages, the subconscious simply takes them in, holding no resistance. This is why it's increasingly important to have the affirmations at such a volume that they're inaudible to the human ear. Of course, this isn't muted. Inaudible refers to a volume that can't be heard over the other music.

Throughout recent years, subliminals have been used for a range of purposes. Many subliminals are posted on video sites and apps such as YouTube, offering audiences a vast selection of subliminals to help with things such as gaining talents, manifesting desires, and obtaining physical changes such as weight loss or eye color transitions. These topics have been incredibly popular within the subliminal community.

The popularity of available online subliminal material led to an increase in videos of users showing off their results from subliminals. Many users report fast results, describing how they've experienced happenings like growing a few inches within a short period of time, or seeing their facial structure change and begin to mold itself into their desired goals.

Alongside the main subliminal message, users may also make use of subliminal "boosters"—shorter length videos employing positive affirmations to increase the efficiency of the subconscious mind's absorbing the message of the main subliminal. These boosters are often placed as the first video in subliminal playlists to ensure listeners are gaining the best results possible and differ from normal videos due to the type of affir-mations used.

# HOW ARE AFFIRMATIONS FORMATTED?

Within the subliminal community, there are common terms and phrases used within video titles to explain to the listener what type of affirmations are being used. Knowing these words and phrases can be incredibly helpful, as it helps you to quickly choose and filter out any subliminals that you don't like or won't find helpful. Remember, everybody's mind works differently, and what works for someone else may not be your cup of tea.

One of the first words to look for is the word *forced*. Forced affirmations are affirmations that are dedicated to people with perhaps a more stubborn and doubtful mind. These affirmations force the listener to take all of the affirmations into their subconscious. In contrast, a normal subliminal may allow a person to pick and choose which affirmations get through, possibly not getting results from a particular affirmation if that's not what they want.

Here's an example of a forced affirmation:

Imagine you're using a subliminal to bring money into your life. The affirmations in this subliminal resonate with you, but one of them says "I receive money from my parents." In this situation, you don't want your parents to give you money, and you'd rather receive it in other ways or from other people. If this were a forced subliminal, you would not be able to separate and block out this affirmation from all the others. Your resistance to it would be stripped bare, the affirmation entering your mind regardless of any doubts or other beliefs you may have. In a normal subliminal, however, you'd be able to simply ignore the affirmation about getting money from your parents and therefore not get results from it. But you would still receive money from all the places you want it, according to the remaining affirmations.

Another term to look out for, which we already briefly touched on, is the word *booster*. Booster subliminals optimize the effects of other subliminals by boosting the results they'll give you in some way. Affirmations used in these booster subliminals follow this type of pattern: "When I blink, I get results a million times faster." Or, "I have full results right now." These are just a couple of examples from a wide pool. Many people use boosters to speed up their results, further opening their minds to positive feelings and improvements.

Now that we have established the types of subliminals and affirmations, we can explore the general rules for how these affirmations are formatted. Despite each subliminal maker being unique and using their own formulas, they often follow specific patterns and come with pieces of advice to help avoid any negative effects or results, and to ensure the affirmations emphasize the best outcomes possible for the subliminal subject.

Firstly, subliminal makers avoid negative words in their affirmations. This includes words such as *don't, not,* and *can't.* This is because our subconscious mind tends to only pick up on negative words, even when there are other positive words in the affirmation. For example, in a phrase such as, "I can't fail my exams," our subconscious focuses on the negative word: *can't.* Despite this affirmation being positive overall, our subconscious may not realize this, and therefore works to produce negative results instead of the positivity we were going for. In order to combat this, subliminal makers establish the negative affirmation, and then work in the opposite direction to make it positive. For example, using the same sentence, instead of "I can't fail my exams," this would be exchanged for "I pass all of my exams."

Affirmations are almost always made in the present tense. During manifestation, we write in the present tense to get rid of the "lack" mindset. The lack mindset occurs when you are focusing more on the lack of an object, feeling, or person rather than imagining you already have what you desire, and therefore, attracting it. Instead of writing affirmations like: "I will get a new pet cat," using "I have a new pet cat" is much more effective because it makes us feel like we already have the cat we desire.

# HOW TO USE
# SUBLIMINALS IN SHIFTING

Subliminals are a great aid to the shifting process. They allow us to alter our mindset into a new one that motivates us and progresses our shift. As with subliminals used for acquiring material things in this reality, like ones used to change your appearance or summon an object, there is an abundance of shifting subliminals. Many of these can be found online, particularly on YouTube.

As you learned in the introduction with the story of choosing between a glass of water or strawberry milkshake, we unknowingly shift millions of times a day. Likewise, when we use any sort of subliminal, we mini-shift when we get results, but we remain unaware due to the unnoticeable and minuscule nature of the shift. Thus, all subliminals are linked to shifting. However, we can also use subliminals specifically tailored to reality shifting in order to achieve the larger shift we desire.

Shifting subliminals usually focus on making the listener feel attached to their desired reality. This facilitates shifters' visualization skills to make them fully resonate with the place they're trying to shift to. In terms of mindset, shifting subliminals can also motivate us to continue making shifting attempts and complete our scripts.

Not only do shifting subliminals push the correct mindset onto the listeners, but they also provide added support to the batch of skills associated with shifting, including focus, meditation, and "method" skills. Shifting subliminals make use of phrases that are highly exaggerated yet highly effective. For example, a subliminal that can help you with meditation could be "I have the best meditation ability in the world." Through use of these subliminals, shifters can improve any weak points in their mindset to bring them closer to their big shift.

As well as general shifting subliminals, there are similarly themed subliminals crafted in a more precise direction, focusing on one specific topic rather than a broad category. There are countless audio recordings out there giving the listener expertise in one or a small number of skills, namely things like ultimate visualization ability, or ultimate meditation ability. Although these themes are also included in normal shifting subliminals, some people may find that they have trouble with one particular skill, such as visualization or meditation. Listening to one specific type of subliminal can help with that.

Below, I've crafted a list of helpful subliminals and subliminal makers to aid you on your journey. These are for a broad range of topics, so hopefully these help you improve your abilities! All of these can be found on YouTube.

## Subliminals for Meditation

◎ Eggtopia's "BREATHE" relaxation meditation and clear conscious subliminal

◎ Eggtopia's "RELEASE" mental health relief subliminal and meditation

◎ Enchanted Workshop's "AVATAR STATE"

◎ CELESTIAL SUBLIMINALS' SHIFTING: just fall asleep and wake up in your DR

## Subliminals for Improving Visualization

◎ Wabbajack Subliminals' forced absolute visualization ability

◎ AKUO's master visualization

◎ Lovegood Subliminals' improve visualization skills for shifting

◎ B1OGENESIS's visualization subliminal

## Subliminals for General Shifting Success

◎ Wabbajack Subliminals' forced revolutionary absolute ideal reality

◎ Angelshyu's desired reality

◎ IASTEARS!'s instant shift subliminal

◎ Lovegood Subliminals' current reality detachment subliminal

◎ Endless Summer reality shifting subliminal

## Subliminal Boosters

○ Wabbajack Subliminals' seamless shifting supplement

○ Wabbajack Subliminals' forced shifting booster

○ Lunare's shifting booster

○ Slyther's Elixirs boost belief in shifting

○ Lovegood Subliminals' shifting subliminal booster

# CHAPTER 8

# METHODS

A shifting method is an exercise we use in order to shift ourselves to our desired reality. Methods can come in a range of styles, from visualization to simple meditation and intention! They can be hard to find online and are often lost in translation from various social media platforms—so this chapter compiles a few well-known methods, including my own (just because I have experience with it, not because I think it's well known and I want to boost my ego a bit, as a quick disclaimer), that you can try out while attempting to shift!

Once again, methods are not for everyone and aren't needed to shift. However, a lot of people do find methods helpful, and it's always worth trying one or two to see if they're right for you.

# SEI METHOD

This is my own method that I posted while using Amino quite often. I actually made this method by accident, as I felt the effects of it while doing meditation. I repeated my steps and found out that I can actually induce this feeling on command. As a result, I made it a method! There are quite a few steps, but hopefully they're easy enough to follow.

One useful tip I'd love to add is that an app called Atmosphere is extremely helpful for this method. Atmosphere is an app that lets you play scenic sounds such as birds chirping or rain, which really help to set the mood for the method and make it easier to get immersed in your visualizations. This isn't a requirement for my method, but it may help if you have trouble visualizing or perhaps have a noisy household.

Now into the method!

**Step 1.** The first step is to make sure your vibrations are high! Watch a TV series or read something that makes you happy. Talk with friends or do whatever makes you feel content to keep your vibes high. Personally, I like to watch videos related to my desired reality in order to make my frequency match with that of the reality I'd like to go to. Doing so makes shifting easier, but this isn't a requirement!

**Step 2.** Once your vibrations are high, lie on your back facing the ceiling. Put your hands at your sides so that they don't touch your body, but keep them close. You may also know this position as the starfish position. You have to be in a comfortable position because you won't move through this whole method. If you have to swallow, that's totally fine!

**Step 3.** Imagine yourself as your desired self in a scenic place. This can be somewhere like a beach or a field (which I often use myself), or it could even be your desired reality or waiting room. Imagine this place however you want it, but make it detailed. Are there any flowers under you? What are you wearing? What would you see if you sat up and looked in front of you? What's behind you? What can you smell? Feel what's under your fingertips. Maybe you're lying on a bed or in a patch of grass, for example. You really need to *feel* where you are, making the visualization as realistic as possible.

**Step 4.** Once you know how the place you're imagining looks and feels, convince yourself that you're genuinely there. Keep visualizing, feel happiness and peace while you're there. This is of utmost importance. Have no doubt in your mind that you're in that place right now because you are.

**Step 5.** The next step depends on time. This will eventually happen, but sadly you just have to wait. For me, this usually happens around five to ten minutes after I've started the method, but it can be different for other people. Be patient and keep waiting! I promise it'll happen.

**Step 6.** After some time, you will feel as if your body is "off." Something on your body will feel weird, like you moved. Usually for me, it's almost like my hand is twisted toward my body, like it is broken, or my neck is tilted when I haven't moved. It doesn't matter what changes, but this means the method is working! This is what we'll refer to as your "second body" leaving your physical body. I use the term "second body" to describe the consciousness leaving your body in this reality and shifting to your desired reality. It's important that no matter what happens, you don't move. Stay still, keep visualizing your place and don't move a centimeter. Don't worry, your body didn't actually move—it's simply a sensation that comes with the method. You are still in the position that you started in, you just *feel* like you've moved.

**Step 7.** This feeling means you can begin the next step! You have to focus on your eyelids. Reinforce that you're still in the place you're visualizing, that hasn't changed, but now you simply have your eyes closed, looking behind your eyelids. If you did it right, you should see colors or patterns moving after a relatively short amount of time. Focus on these patterns and follow them with your eyes wherever they move. I usually see green stripes that move from left to right. It's important to keep your eyes closed, and to make sure you aren't opening your eyes slightly, which can often happen during methods.

**Step 8.** Keep doing this until you feel your body shake. It'll feel light at first, but after a while you'll feel your heart beating faster, and you'll get a side-to-side tipping sensation. It's increasingly important that you focus on your breathing. If you can't control it, the shaking will stop, and it's really difficult to do the method again. Breathe slowly and put all your focus on your breathing. If the shaking stops, try holding your breath and see if it comes back! When it does, stabilize your breathing again while trying to keep a hold of the feeling. Once again, your physical body isn't moving at all. This shaking isn't happening physically and is more a sensation that only feels like your body is moving when it really isn't. While you're still breathing, the shaking will become stronger. To be honest, it's a bit of a shock while practicing the method for the first time, how much and how fast you're "moving"—it's hard to understand. Don't let this stop you from doing the method though. I can assure you it's completely safe and harmless!

**Step 9.** To shift to your desired reality, keep focusing on the colors behind your eyelids. You'll start to see a white light and you should move along with the method. While you see the white, affirm that you're shifting (affirmations such as "I am pure consciousness allowing myself to shift to my desired reality," "I am in my desired reality right now") and remember your desired reality in terms of visualization before your vision is completely over. For a lot of people, this light takes over your vision, leading to the shift. This light should be very bright (at least in my experience!) and you won't mistake it for anything else. Simply make sure your eyes are completely shut, as some people doing the method accidentally begin opening their eyes slightly, letting light in, leading them to believe *this* is the white light. If you don't see this white light after quite a long time or don't shift immediately after seeing it and it disappears, I'd recommend trying to fall asleep in this same position while affirming you've shifted.

That's all for the method explanation! A lot of people seem to have a few questions and misconceptions about it, so I'll quickly list a few here before moving on to the next method.

First, this method is completely painless and safe. If you're feeling any form of pain or discomfort during these steps, this is *not* because of the method. If any problems occur for you, I'd highly recommend changing methods and going to see a doctor.

You may also wonder, "How do I know I've shifted?" When you see the light, you may feel a change of atmosphere, such as a different smell taking over your senses, new touch under your fingers, or a noise you hear that wasn't there previously. If you feel your atmosphere change, you've shifted! It's hard to mistake the feeling of shifting, so if you feel as if you've shifted, I'd definitely recommend taking the risk and opening your eyes to check.

# ELEVATOR METHOD

The elevator method is one of the first methods popularized online years ago. This method gained popularity on Amino and many began using it to successfully shift.

**Step 1.** The first step is to imagine yourself in this reality in an elevator. Imagine this elevator however you want, but try and visualize it as realistically as possible. Imagine the sliding doors opening, the metal paneling, even the soft elevator music playing in the background. Once you get inside the elevator, the doors shut. Press the one hundredth floor, and the elevator will start moving.

**Step 2.** Visualize a number going up in the elevator, indicating which floor you're on. With each floor, feel your energy levels getting higher and higher. If you're struggling to do this, try to feel energy in one part of your body to start off—your hands, for example. With each floor, make the energy spread further and further around your body. It doesn't matter which way you spread the energy during the method, as long as it's increasing with each floor.

**Step 3.** Congratulations! You've reached the top floor. The doors have to open, and you'll get out. Visualize being in your desired reality as your desired self. This can be anywhere, but make sure there's a place to sleep here—your bedroom, for example. Turn into your desired self as you step out and take in the scenes around you. Touch the walls when you get out and take in the smell alongside all the other senses. What do you feel now that you're in your desired reality? Incorporate this feeling into your visualization.

**Step 4.** Lastly, all you need to do is walk over to the place to sleep and lie down. Imagine falling asleep in your desired reality while simultaneously falling asleep in this reality. When you wake up, you will have shifted there!

# RAVEN METHOD

This is one of the most popular and well-known methods online! Many people have shifted with this one. For this method, you have to lie in the starfish position once again. It's also recommended that you're half asleep, so consider doing a meditation or getting yourself tired before starting!

**Step 1.** Get yourself into the starfish position.

**Step 2.** Next, count from one to one hundred. Focus on steady breathing while doing so, and say one affirmation with each number. For example, you may use affirmations such as "I am my own universe" or "I am shifting/I have shifted." Feel free to repeat any of these affirmations as you work your way through the method.

**Step 3.** This step is optional, as some people don't prefer to visualize. If you find that visualization helps you, on each tenth number, try to visualize your desired reality. If you don't enjoy visualization, try to focus on the feeling and happiness you'll experience when you're in your desired reality.

**Step 4.** Hopefully, you'll have shifted with the method when you reach one hundred! If not, you have the option to keep counting up to the next hundred and repeating the steps, or fall asleep while doing so.

# SUNNI METHOD

This method has been around for as long as I can remember and was actually the most well-known method around the time I started shifting. It's perfect for those who are good at visualizing and is a fairly easy method with minimal steps.

The point of the Sunni method is to force yourself to believe in your desired reality. This can be done wherever you are, from in school to lying in bed. For example, imagine that you're sitting in a chair during a class. Instead of accepting the fact you're in class, visualize yourself sitting in a chair in your desired reality. Attempt to make any noises from this reality link with your desired reality; for example, a noisy classroom while you're in a lesson could be turned into the noise in a busy cafe. No matter where you are, imagine you're in the same situation as your desired self.

This method is one you can practice multiple times a day, whenever you have free time. Not only can this help you shift, but it can also massively improve your visualization skills if you feel as if that's something you may benefit from working on.

# ROPE METHOD

This is another method that gained popularity a few years ago, leading to many successful shifts as detailed in a range of Amino communities. This method is one I liked to use when I first began shifting.

**Step 1.** Imagine you're in a dark, incredibly high setting, the ceiling so far up you struggle to see it from below. Everything around you is pitch black. But as you look up, you see a hole with light shining down and illuminating a rope. This rope is stretching all the way from the high ceiling to where you stand on the floor below. The top of the rope is extremely high up, and the only way you can reach the light is to climb it.

**Step 2.** Lie down below the rope. The rope should be hanging just above the middle of your body.

**Step 3.** Imagine your consciousness coming out of your body lying under the rope, and begin to climb the rope as your consciousness. As you climb up, keep in mind that you're crawling to the light. Realize as you get higher that the light is your desired reality, and when you reach the top, you'll shift. Feel the pure happiness as you get higher and higher.

**Step 4.** Once you hit the top, get out of the dark hole you were in. You're now in your desired reality! Look around—it's your bedroom or a similar place where you can see your desired self sleeping.

**Step 5.** Walk over to your desired self's body and merge your consciousness with this body. Visualize your consciousness becoming one with this body.

**Step 6.** If you don't shift immediately, repeat the method as you fall asleep!

# TV METHOD

This method is one that keeps a focus on your feelings, reminding you of past, present, and future experiences in your script to raise your vibration in order to shift.

**Step 1.** Visualize yourself sitting in your living room in this reality. Turn the TV on.

**Step 2.** The first channel you come across is one showing a memory from your desired reality. This memory should be something from the past in your desired reality, perhaps from your childhood.

**Step 3.** Change the channel once more, and the next channel will show what will happen the day you shift. Don't think about waking up and shifting, but imagine what your first day will be like.

**Step 4.** Once again, change the channel. This channel will show something that will happen in the future of your desired reality. Watch it play out and fully feel what's happening, as if you're reacting to a show. Is it making you feel happy, or maybe excited?

**Step 5.** Lastly, one more channel change. In this one, you're finally waking up in your desired reality. See your desired body lying down in bed.

**Step 6.** Put your hand up to the TV screen. As your hand touches the screen, it goes through! Pull your whole body through the same way and enter the TV channel. You're now in your desired bedroom, or wherever you have scripted that you'll wake up when you shift.

**Step 7.** Lie down in the same place your desired body is. Do this in a way that your body merges into theirs.

**Step 8.** You've shifted! Now fall asleep as your desired self.

# 369 METHOD

The 369 method is an extremely well-established one, gaining traction on a range of different platforms. This method is widely known for manifestation of desires but can also be used for affirmations throughout the day to help us shift.

**Step 1.** To do this method, you first need to write out a longer affirmation. This affirmation should take around twenty seconds to write out. An example of an affirmation would be "I am pure consciousness and my own universe. I can shift at my own will and all of the power of the universe is within me. I have shifted."

**Step 2.** Now that you have this method, you must repeat it throughout the day. This is where the numbers come in. In the morning, you should write out the affirmation three times. In the evening, you repeat it six times, followed by nine times in the evening. This can be done on paper or typed out, but make sure it takes around twenty seconds for either medium.

# LUCID DREAMING METHOD

This method will first require you to have a lucid dream. As stated in Chapter 2, writing down your dreams as soon as you wake up and consistently performing reality checks will help induce lucid dreams. However, this won't work for immediate success. Instead, it is more of a buildup toward your goal. If you're looking to lucid dream, it may be worth trying one of these methods.

The first method is to wake up after around five hours of sleep using an alarm, and then to fall back asleep afterward. While you fall asleep for the second time, tell yourself that you're going to realize you're in a dream when you're asleep. Keep this thought in your mind until you eventually drift off. If this doesn't work for you, try staying awake for thirty minutes to an hour before falling asleep again.

Another way you may be able to induce a lucid dream is by tricking your brain into believing you're asleep. When you get into bed, make sure you're comfy. You don't want to be too tired, as you'll have to stay awake for a while with your eyes closed. Close your eyes and focus on staying awake. While you do this, make sure that you don't move your body an inch. Ignore any sort of itch you get and simply remain still. After a while, your body will be the same as it is during your sleep, and you may find yourself unable to move. This is the prime state for a lucid dream, as your brain is still awake, yet your body is still. Once you've followed these steps, a lucid dream should begin, an image forming in front of you.

There aren't many steps to this method once you're aware you're in a lucid dream. When you're dreaming, stay calm and don't let your emotions get the best of you. Now you're here, you need to imagine a portal forming in front of you. This can be any sort of portal you want, but the portal has to shift you to your desired reality. Step through this portal and find yourself there! If you haven't shifted immediately, affirm that you have now shifted, or fall asleep in your desired reality inside the dream while you continue to affirm.

# CREATING YOUR OWN METHOD

Methods come in a range of different shapes and forms, utilizing different techniques such as visualization, meditation, or lucid dreaming to eventually shift the user as the main goal. However, methods, may not always help you the way they're intended to, and you could find that part of one method works, yet the rest gives you no results as all. Perhaps you find that sleep methods are easiest for you (when you're asked to fall asleep for the method to work) but you may struggle to visualize.

This is a reason why making your own method may be extremely beneficial to you. By doing this you can craft your own routine, making use of all the things that are easiest for you and that give you results to make the optimal shifting method.

If this interests you, the first thing I'd suggest you do is give a few different methods a try. Try to use different techniques so you're trying something new in each one.

Make a note of what seems to give you the most results, if any (remember, you don't *need* method, to shift; they aren't everyone's cup of tea), or note simply what you're good at or what you're most comfortable doing. From here you can put a new method together.

Let's say you now have one or two things that really seem to work for you, or that you feel quite comfortable and confident doing. You can use or combine these to make your method. When thinking about a method, I'd recommend implementing something that you know will make you feel happy and raise your vibrations. For example, if you're using visualization in your method, what can you visualize that will make you the most determined to shift? If you're meditating, which meditation makes you feel comfortable? By using these, the shifting process will become just that bit easier.

Once you're done, all that's left to do is use it! You could even give it a name if you'd like.

# CHAPTER 9

# DREAM MEANINGS

Our mind is extremely complex—a hive of information containing memories that even we can't voluntarily bring to the surface.

Think of our minds as an iceberg, as demonstrated by Freud. This example is overused, but it works perfectly in describing exactly how information is stored. The conscious mind is the tip of the iceberg, it's slightly above the water and we can see this part very clearly. Due to the conscious being above the water, we can bring anything from this part of our minds to the surface. This consists of things such as basic information like names and dates to conscious needs and desires, such as itching to get something to eat or a glass of water when you're thirsty.

A little lower is the subconscious. This part of the mind is submerged under the water but isn't too deep just yet. Since the subconscious is underwater, it's a bit harder to bring information from here to the surface. It's a struggle to do this voluntarily, and we often have to be prompted to recall information from here. For example, when somebody brings up a memory that you haven't thought about in many years, it's then fresh in your mind once more. The very bottom of the iceberg is in dark water, hidden completely from our conscious thought process and inaccessible. The unconscious holds the baseline for our behavior as a human being, influencing our decisions and actions.

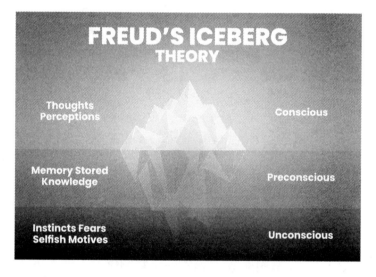

We dream the most during REM (rapid eye movement) stages of our sleep, where the brain is nearly as active as it is when we're awake. Despite being able to dream in any stage of our sleep, the increased brain activity that comes with REM causes our brains to come up with these images, thoughts, and feelings we have in our dreams.

As evidenced by the iceberg model, the human mind hides emotions, knowledge about the self, and wise advice we can take to move forward in our lives and let go of any blockages or negative feelings. But how do we get these to come to the surface?

Information coming to us in dreams is actually one of the key ways in which the subconscious can communicate with the conscious mind.

The reason we dream and the true essence of them is something scientists are still trying to fully figure out to this day. Although we have a grasp on sleep cycles, the difference in REM sleep compared to other sleep stages, and the importance of REM to the likelihood of having and remembering a dream, we are still unsure exactly why our mind comes up with these vivid, complex story lines while we rest. Many believe that dreams are the brain's way of recounting our day, and reaffirming any information or feelings we remember or experience in our waking life. Dreaming could also be thought of as a way of cleaning out your mind, filtering through memories we need and getting rid of ones we don't. Others also believe dreams are a key way of confronting emotions that we may struggle with in our waking lives. Being asleep helps to shed light on our feelings without being blurred by waking logic.

The last interpretation is what we're focusing on in this chapter: explaining common themes and symbolism in dreams and how these can expose hidden emotions.

Interpreting your dreams is helpful for your shifting journey, as we can often find ourselves in a dead end situation. Maybe you've been trying different methods, but none seem to fit you correctly, or perhaps you're feeling like something in this reality is holding you back, but don't know what it is! With this chapter, you'll gain a better insight on how to move forward and finally shift, and this information will be handed to you by your own mind during your dreams.

# HOW TO ANALYZE A DREAM

The baseline of analyzing a dream actually lies within you.

Our dreams are a window into our subconscious troubles and worries, exposing the feelings that we may not be consciously aware of. Somebody can ask you what your dream is and give you an interpretation based on that, but what you'll notice is that some parts may fit while others may not. This is because the person doing the interpretation is not inside your mind. How would they know your fears, past experiences, stresses, and worries? You, yourself, are the best person to analyze your own dreams, and it's a lot simpler than you think! You don't need anything fancy such as a book or any form of education on the matter, and it can be done with just a phone and some internet research.

Let's assume you've remembered or written down your dream in as much detail as you can possibly recall. I'd recommend that shifters do this, as it gives an insight on any improvements you can make to your mindset while shifting. You can remember some information such as the people in your dream and the colors of the clothes they were wearing. It's also fine if you don't remember this much detail. Whatever you can recall will be enough to give you an insight on the dream's meaning.

I'm going to give a tutorial on how to interpret your dream's meaning through an example of my own—a quick trigger warning for gun violence.

Back when I was in high school, I had repeated dreams of somebody taking a gun and killing people inside the school. Sometimes the shooter was a man I didn't know, but other times it was actually me. I specifically remember losing a sock in one of these dreams and feeling scared to go back and get it. I remembered these dreams in vivid detail and could actually sometimes smell what was going on in the dreams. During these times, I was extremely stressed with school due to having to deal with a boy there who was making me highly uncomfortable (this detail links in later).

So far we have a few pieces of information: the dream is set in school, there were shootings going on, and sometimes I was the shooter, other times I wasn't. Do the same with your dream. Try to pick out the basic fundamental pieces that make up your dream.

Now that you have your basic information of the dream, try searching each individual thing online to get a few different interpretations. I would advise you to check a few different websites, as different signs can have varied meanings, and I'd also recommend looking into popular dream theorists such as Jung and Freud.

For my dream, I'm going to start with the gun, as they were dreams about shootings. The first thing I stumbled across is that guns can be representative of masculinity and the male sexuality as a phallocentric symbol, but they may also suggest powerlessness when someone else is holding it. My using the gun could imply I desired total control of a situation.

When a place you're familiar with comes up in a dream, it's best to think about how that place makes you feel in your waking life because it could impact the meaning of the dream. If the place in your dream is unfamiliar or you have no particular feelings toward it, it's still advisable to look online for any possible meanings surrounding this place. School made me feel extremely stressed. Linking this to the gun, it implies I may have either felt stressed due to a male presence or that I wanted to feel powerful in a situation where I felt small.

Lastly, there's the sock detail. Socks can symbolize comfort and warmth due to their being a form of protective footwear. But in the dream, I actually ended up losing my sock inside the school. The fact that I lost it signifies that I'd been stripped away of feelings of comfort when inside that building.

Summarizing all the points I've collected from these recurring dreams, it suggests that I felt stressed or undermined by a male presence because I was losing my comfort when at school and that I wanted to regain power over the situation. All of this is true! This is exactly how I was feeling at the time. Luckily, this situation got sorted out and the dreams stopped.

You'll likely have quite a few different interpretations for each object, place, or person you're researching. While this may be confusing at first, a theme should become quite evident once you've figured out the meanings of a few! Spot similarities between the interpretations and try to tie them into your feelings and other parts of your dream. Once you've done this, you'll start to see the rest of the signs from your dream have interpretations following the theme you've established. It's then easier to put together a narrative of how you're feeling in your conscious life, your doubts, worries, or joys coming to the surface.

# MOST COMMON DREAM SYMBOLS

Each dream is highly intricate and unique, with no person's brain working in exactly the same way as another. Dreams are also unique because many of us don't have the same experiences or emotions impacting the type of dream we're having. Despite this, there are common types of dreams with particular happenings that many people have. A few examples of these sorts of dreams are ones in which you or somebody you know is dying, you're falling from a high place, or you're being chased by somebody in a nightmare. All of these are a lot more common than you think, and all of these symbols are actually what give your dreams a meaning.

Below is a list of a few of the most common events during dreams paired with their meanings. These will be linked to shifting in some shape or form, but the normal definition will also be there, free for you to use for any day-to-day dreams interpretation you may want to try.

# DEATH

Dreaming about death may seem cruel and heart-breaking in nature and may force you to wake up worried the dream was some sort of precognitive warning. Whenever I've woken up after dreaming about death, I've definitely felt a sense of unease. But worry not! Dreaming about death can actually be a great thing—especially if you're thinking about shifting.

Death often symbolizes a fresh start, or the "death" of a part of your mind or personality. This is dependent on the context in which you died in the dream. How did you die? Looking at this will give you more of an insight on exactly why this new start needed to happen. On a more negative note, dreaming of death can also expose frustrations you have during your waking life and a need to escape these. Perhaps you died in school, or you were murdered by a close friend that you actually have negative feelings toward. Situations like this can indicate what needs to be worked on or taken out of your life to avoid this stress.

In shifting terms, death means a new beginning. Dreaming of death as a shifter is an amazing sign you're doing something right, as your mind can acknowledge you're striving for a fresh start, a rebirth almost.

## FALLING

The first thing we need to establish with falling dreams is that they could be prompted by a fear of heights or falling in your waking life. We can't easily let go of our fears, and this gives our brains more of a chance to cling to them and make us face them while asleep. These aren't memories that may be buried deep in your mind, but fears that have been haunting us for long periods of time. If you've perhaps seen a piece of media recently involving heights, or someone falling from any sort of height, whether this is big or small, this may have been on your mind subconsciously and acted out during your dream. Even if you didn't clock this while you were awake, remember that your subconscious remembers everything you're taking in. I always find it common to dream about insignificant things during my day, so this may be the same for you. Not only does this apply to dreams where you're falling from somewhere, but also other dreams where you may have subconsciously remembered an event on something like TV or social media.

If you aren't scared of falling, your dream may be trying to give you a message. Falling is often associated with a loss of control. When falling from a high place, we're rendered powerless in the situation and just have to let it happen for it to be over. If this is the case, it's important to consider exactly where you were falling from and how it happened. For example, you may have been falling from the roof of your workplace in your dream. If you add the loss of control factor to the workplace, this indicates that you could be feeling powerless at work, or that you have no control over your work life. If you've fallen and something has interrupted or broken the fall, it's also worth thinking about why that happened. Maybe someone caught you, suggesting you have positive or reassuring feelings toward that person in your waking life. More things to consider are if somebody pushed you, if you tripped over something, if you jerked awake after falling—or did the dream continue?

In terms of shifting, falling once again suggests loss of control in your current reality. If you do dream about falling, it could be worth considering if you're feeling lost on your shifting journey, or like you're incapable of shifting. Do you feel like you're losing control over whether you shift or not? If so, look at the rest of the dream and fish out any other symbols to actively combat these feelings and further your journey.

## BEING CHASED

Being followed during a dream is never a good feeling. If you take note of your pounding heart and your nervousness when hiding from the chaser, you may realize these feelings can be similar to some anxieties in your waking life. Being chased often reveals that something is once again stressing you out during your waking life, following you around, and causing you to run away and avoid this problem. Interpreting this dream would depend on who exactly the attacker is and what they represent. If they're a family member, you may have some conflict or negative emotions to resolve surrounding them. The same goes for any other people you know personally in real life. But what if you don't know who the chaser is?

If you're unaware of who the chaser is, it's more about what they represent. The first thing to think about is *where* you're being chased. After that, are they wearing anything that stands out? Maybe they have a recognizable weapon with them, or certain physical features. What gender are they? How are they chasing you? Are they looking to attack you, or are they simply chasing you around? Did anything happen prior to your being chased? All of these factors will help you come to terms with what the chaser is a symbol of, and exposing what your troubles in your waking life are. Look at the smaller symbols (such as the weapon), find out the meaning, and then simply apply it.

As a shifter, something stressing you out in this reality could be a reason you're struggling to shift for a multitude of reasons. Perhaps you're struggling to focus due to your mind worrying, or you don't have time to even think about shifting because of complications here. If you're being chased in your dream, try and act on what your dream is telling you. Sorting out a stressful situation may work in your favor.

## FLYING

Another extremely common experience in dreams is flying. Like other interpretations, flying may represent your own sense of power. If you're flying high in wide open space, this suggests that you're currently feeling a sense of freedom. Maybe you just finished a set of exams and are now free to spend your time how you want, or perhaps you got out of a friendship that was holding you down. But what if you're flying low and unable to go higher? If something is stopping you from truly flying free, this means something may be holding you down from freedom in your waking life. The same goes for anything obstructing your path, such as birds, clouds, or street poles.

In shifting terms, the *way* you're flying could indicate how you're feeling about shifting at this current time. If you're flying high and free, this implies that shifting has given you a good escape and you're appreciating the journey. You know you'll be out of your current reality soon, and maybe you feel enlightened. If you're struggling to get to that height or you're unable to fly well, something may be holding you back from shifting. Clearly, your mind does know what this is. But if you're unsure on what this could be, look at more symbols during the dream. Some examples of other things that could be holding you back from shifting success are a connection to this reality, procrastination, or stress.

## PUBLIC HUMILIATION

Being naked during a dream is extremely common, leaving the dreamer feeling exposed and embarrassed in front of the dream's public. The main thing dreams like this give us is insight into an insecurity. Not only does this apply to being naked, but also any other type of humiliation in public, such as being made fun of in front of a crowd or doing something embarrassing. If you're around people you know, such as a group of friends, that shows you may feel inferior to them. Dreaming about being naked or embarrassed in front of strangers could show you feel inferior to other people in general, or maybe you're a self-conscious individual.

As previously mentioned, these sorts of dreams give us a picture of what's making us insecure in ourselves. Look for other signs and symbols in your dream. If any of these seem to relate to shifting or a new beginning, think about what the dream is telling you—perhaps what you're insecure about. Remember you're an extremely powerful individual, and you can gradually work on easing these insecurities!

## DRIVING

This type of dream is pretty self-evident! If you're driving, your dream interpretation depends on whether you're in control of the car or not, and what your destination is. If you're in control of the car, that can suggest you're in control of your waking life, or perhaps your shifting journey. Losing control of the car suggests the opposite—that you feel like you're losing control over certain aspects of your life or shifting journey. A car crash is representative of similar themes. It's worth once again looking around for other symbols of whether you've lost control, in order to figure out what can be worked on or changed in your waking life for your happiness and progress.

# RECALLING YOUR DREAMS

Did you know that we forget approximately 90 percent of our dreams? We can dream multiple times a night, but most of the time we actually end up forgetting these. More often than not, when we wake up, we only seem to remember one of our dreams, and the dream is usually in a continuous storyline. When we wake up, the chemicals our brain uses during our sleep begin to fade away. These are the chemicals that allow us to vividly experience our dreams, but they just as quickly lead our brains to forgetting the events that happened during our sleep.

There is, however, a way to train ourselves to remember our dreams more often, and even dream more during our sleep. This method also increases our chances of having a lucid dream.

We do this by writing down our dreams in as much detail as possible.

Sounds easy, right? When you wake up, try to write down as much as you can possibly remember within five minutes. After five minutes, that dream will begin to fade from your memory. Even if you wake up for a few minutes after a dream and it's an ungodly hour in the morning, keep a journal or your phone by your bed so you can write down the dream before falling asleep again. That way you won't regret not doing so in the morning when you can no longer recall your dream. You can record your dreams on pen and paper, or you can use an app. There are several apps in the app store that are tailored specifically for writing down your dreams after they happen, and then storing them, safe and organized. A couple of good apps for this are Lucid - Dream Journal and Somnio: Dream Journal.

After having written the dream down, you should notice that when you reread it you can actually recall the dream in vivid color and detail. The images will seem much clearer in your head than if you didn't write it down and stuck to plain old memory. There will even be details you wouldn't have remembered if you hadn't written them down! By doing this, it's now easier to analyze the dream with all the components in front of you, whether big or small. You now remember all the details you'd possibly need to get an accurate reading of your mind's sleepy storyline. Additionally, this method of recording your dreams is used by people wanting to lucid dream. If you write down your dreams whenever you wake up remembering one, you're more likely to lucid dream the more often you do this.

All in all, analyzing your dreams can tell you more about yourself than you'd be aware of while awake. Nobody knows you better than yourself; your brain sheds light onto smaller details you don't pick up on regarding your hidden fears and emotions.

While shifting, we sometimes hit a slump that can feel like a dead end. We may be losing motivation, or be finding that nothing seems to be working out. Your dreams can give you an insight about what to improve on and what may be causing a blockage. You can't dive into your subconscious and figure out what to do next while awake, but by analyzing symbols in your dreams, your subconscious will expose your true feelings and next steps.

# CHAPTER 10

# THE PLACEBO EFFECT

Have you ever tricked yourself into having a physical response to your thoughts? For example, getting a headache after thinking about having one. Or possibly a more psychological response, learning a new word and then noticing it around you constantly for days afterward? Our mind works in such a way that we can have a tangible response as a consequence of our thoughts.

The placebo effect is a classic example of this. We often hear of the placebo effect when it's used in scientific trials, usually for things like testing the efficacy of a certain medicinal drug. The way it works is that a portion of test participants receive the real drug and are monitored to see the effects it has on a person. However, the remaining participants are given a fake drug, or a "placebo." This is not a drug at all and would have no real effect on the participant, yet they're still monitored in order to compare their experiences with the people who took the real drug during the test. The participants have no idea if they received the real drug or a placebo, making the test fair and genuine.

In past experiments, researchers have found that many of the placebo participants actually reported that the "drug" was working on them in some way. Sometimes both the placebo participants and the real drug participants even reported having the same effects from the drug they had taken. At present, researchers have determined that this may not mean that the trial drug doesn't work, but that the placebo participant's minds actually formulated a response to the "drug." The placebo participant saw that other participants, the ones who received the real drug, were being affected by the drug, so their minds made their bodies feel like they too were experiencing the same effects. Here we see that due to the belief and mindset of the placebo participant, the body was affected by the person's consciousness. This was termed the placebo effect.

Another example of the placebo effect is pseudocyesis, often referred to as "false pregnancy." In some cases, women are led to believe they're pregnant and encounter countless symptoms of pregnancy such as weight gain, nausea, missed periods, and even sensations of fetal movement within the body. It's suspected that psychological factors may be the cause of these false sensations and side effects, fooling the body into displaying all the relevant signs of pregnancy. False pregnancy could happen for many reasons, but the most prominent explanation stems from the desire to become pregnant. Depending on a woman's past with issues such as infertility or miscarriages, or perhaps simply chemical imbalances within the body, she may have an intense longing to become pregnant. These psychological longings are then transformed into physical signs of pregnancy due to the placebo effect.

Despite there being no concrete explanation for the existence of the placebo effect, there are some possible explanations for how it works.

One of these is classical conditioning (also known as Pavlovian conditioning)—two stimuli linked together to generate a response. This is evidenced in an experiment led by Pavlov himself, when he investigated the way in which dogs learned to associate one stimulus with another. In this experiment, Pavlov measured the amount of saliva generated by dogs when faced with stimuli that reminded them of food; for example, the footsteps of somebody walking in to feed them. Pavlov realized that the dogs had the same response when confronted with any event reminding them of food. He even created a brand-new stimulus to remind the dogs of food: Pavlov would ring a bell before feeding the dogs. Over time, the dogs linked the sound of the bell to the thought of food. So even when the bell was rung and it wasn't time for food, the dogs still salivated and wanted food because they had learned that the bell meant food.

In conclusion, the dogs learned to link two stimuli in their minds—food and the sound of a bell—and therefore, this mental connection caused a physical effect: the dog salivated when he heard a bell. Another example of classical conditioning once again leads back to medicinal drugs. If we take drugs to treat a specific problem such as pains in the body, we eventually associate the drugs with pain relief. This encourages the placebo effect in our minds as we take the drug, because we have a subsequent expectation of the effects the drug is supposed to have on us. It's been found that when a patient expects a treatment to work, the chances of it genuinely working are higher than someone who has a negative and doubtful mindset toward the same treatment.

Another way the placebo effect is thought to work is through the expectations of the subject and how they believe something will work for them. For example, a patient who believes the medicine that they're taking will work well for them is more likely to experience a positive placebo effect than another patient who has low hopes for that medication.

# THE PLACEBO EFFECT IN SHIFTING

But how does the placebo effect relate to shifting?

The shifting process requires a good mindset, as negative thoughts and subconscious doubts can often draw back people's shifting journeys. These doubts and negative emotions can be brought to the surface and acknowledged through dreams and meditation, as detailed in Chapters 6 and 7. Employing a mindset similar to the placebo effect during shifting can push us to achieve the positive mindset needed to shift. As stated previously, when we have a positive expectation of the results, these results are more likely to manifest in real life.

By constantly convincing yourself that you're going to shift throughout the day, you can set this result in stone in your mind, and ultimately make the shifting process easier. An effective way to do so is by setting a daily routine to stick to, taking time out of your day in regular intervals to visualize or affirm your shifting goals.

I, myself, have an experience with the placebo effect leading to a near-shift experience, although I was not fully intending to shift that night. On this night in particular, I was planning to meditate before sleeping. As I was getting ready for bed, I briefly remembered telling myself I was going to shift during the meditation. Sure enough, near the end of the meditation, I began seeing a blinding white light taking over my vision, a shaking sensation engulfing my body. I personally find that saying an affirmation once or twice and then completely forgetting my intention works the best for me, but each person's mind works in different ways. What works for another person may not be the correct route for you.

# HOW TO MAKE A ROUTINE

Making yourself an affirmation routine throughout the day requires self-discipline and good time management, as well as an awareness of how your mind works and what's best for it. Similar to the 369 method (explained in more detail in Chapter 8), setting aside some time multiple times a day to set an intention—or in this case, an expectation—may increase the likelihood of shifting.

First, what works best for you? Perhaps you're a full-time student and only have time in the morning and at night. Maybe you have a lot of free time and can condition your mind every hour. Both of these routines work just as well as the other, and there are no set rules on how to make your own routine.

Here's an example of a routine in which you would remind yourself you're going to shift at each hour change. Pick a specific hour, then whenever the clock hits that exact hour, reinforce the idea that you're intensely talented in shifting and it's a completely natural process you've been utilizing your entire life. Tell yourself that tonight, you're going to shift to your desired reality. Even sentences as simple as these are enough to correctly condition your mind and induce the placebo effect to heighten your shifting skills.

For people with less time on their hands, another routine example is repeating these sentences in your mind for a few minutes in the morning and sometime later in the afternoon. The key to this routine method isn't how often you do it, but the effectiveness of the affirmations you're repeating, and the impact these have on your subconscious and conscious mind.

Here's a chart to fill in! You can use this to make yourself a routine and plan out any times you'd like to repeat affirmations to aid you on your shifting journey.

## 12-Hour Shifting Routine

| HOUR | SHIFTING AFFIRMATIONS |
|---|---|
| __ __ : __ __ | |
| __ __ : __ __ | |
| __ __ : __ __ | |
| __ __ : __ __ | |
| __ __ : __ __ | |
| __ __ : __ __ | |
| __ __ : __ __ | |
| __ __ : __ __ | |

| HOUR | SHIFTING AFFIRMATIONS |
|---|---|
| __ __ : __ __ | |
| __ __ : __ __ | |
| __ __ : __ __ | |
| __ __ : __ __ | |

## Daily Shifting Routine

| TIME OF DAY | SHIFTING AFFIRMATIONS |
|---|---|
| Morning | |
| Afternoon | |
| Night | |

# CHAPTER 11

# CLOSING THOUGHTS

So you've found out about shifting and made it this far through the book—congratulations! You now have all the knowledge you could possibly need on how to shift, and all that's left is to finally push forward and do it. However, for some people this is the hardest part of the journey. Scripting is fun and relatively simple. It gets you excited about where you're going to be in the future. Finding methods to try is also an entertaining activity because there are so many to choose from, ranging from ones involving visualization to full-blown shifting routines. The actual shifting aspect, on the other hand, can seem fairly daunting, especially for people who haven't shifted before.

This is completely understandable! Shifting is a new experience. When we first find out about the concept, it seems too good to be true, which often makes us wonder if what we're doing and all the effort we're putting in will pay off in the end. I get it—scripting can be tiresome at times, especially for those who spend hours reading through material and fine-tuning their scripts to ensure that they're absolutely perfect. The doubts and worries we get when the newfound enthusiasm gradually slips away are unavoidable, yet can put a significant pause on our shifting journey.

Each person will find doubts around different aspects of shifting, depending on the level of importance that has to them. A personal example is scripting, which placed a lot of worries in my mind when I first started trying to shift.

My scripts for the first reality I wanted to shift to were extensive (an understatement) to say the least. I was writing pages upon pages solely on my appearance, going into extreme detail on exactly how my lips looked, how my eyes sparkled in the sun—tiny little things like this. Due to the nature of what I was writing, I was stressed that everything wouldn't appear exactly as I wanted it in my desired reality when I shifted there. In order to prevent this, I started limiting what I was writing down, and I'd obsessively read over my scripts and repeat the smaller sentences in my head to make sure they stuck. This obviously was very tiresome and didn't end up working. My mind was just as empty as it was when I started, and I became more and more hesitant to do my chosen method and shift for fear of its not being *perfect*.

I struggled to find anybody who shared the same doubts as me, so it was hard to get it out of my head since nobody reaffirmed the stupidity of it. I held onto this false belief for months until one day, I had a realization that I already knew the answer to my own worry. I'd held onto the knowledge that our subconscious remembers minuscule happenings from our day-to-day lives, such as faces our conscious mind doesn't even pick up on when we walk past a group of strangers. I had dreams where memories from my past were brought back to the surface, but the funny thing was that I didn't even remember these events until my subconscious placed them right in front of my eyes while I was asleep. My mind drifted back to my use of subliminals, and how they work due to the subconscious recognizing the inaudible affirmations behind the music.

I realized that the subconscious remembers every single detail, no matter how useless or trivial my mind believed they were. Automatically, the weight was lifted off my shoulders and I could easily let go of this idea of having everything perfect.

Overcoming doubts surrounding your shifting journey may not be that simple and could be more of a gradual change of a negative mindset. But it's not impossible and might just take time!

Arguably, the most common doubt I've noticed people have encountered is the general doubt about shifting, having second thoughts on the reality of it, and whether it's a genuinely possible goal. Releasing the doubt temporarily is quite straightforward—we can sometimes push it to the back of our minds and continue with our shifting journey despite this setback. However, sometimes this just isn't quite enough. Not believing in the actions you're doing can have a larger impact than you'd expect and can often make us hesitate on doing something, such as a method or a routine, out of fear that we won't shift after doing it.

This, alongside many other ideas popping up in our heads, can prevent us from shifting.

Overall, despite the hardships that may come with working past your doubts, shifting is a one-of-a-kind experience and a journey like no other. When you're feeling down, simply remind yourself what all this work is for.

We all have doubts, but there's no better way to permanently get rid of these than to shift ourselves. Just go do it! There's no need to rely on others when you're just as capable and could go and shift right now. Each attempt we make, we only get closer.

As said previously, there's no experience quite like this. This is your chance to live a life that many dream of. Shifting is an extremely positive experience that brings me and many others so much joy and peace..

I wish you the best of luck on your journey!

# RESOURCES

## SOCIAL MEDIA

**Amino – Desired Reality**

https://aminoapps.com/c/desiredrealiity

A group on the social media platform Amino, where you can find fellow shifters and information about all aspects of reality shifting.

## APPS

**Atmosphere**

https://apps.apple.com/us/app/atmosphere-relaxing-sounds/id1259186300

This app lets you play scenic, white noise sounds such as birds chirping or rain falling. It is very useful for setting the mood to do methods or immerse yourself in your visualizations. I use it when doing my own shifting method (Sei's Method).

**Lucid – Dream Journal**

https://play.google.com/store/apps/details?id=fm.lucid.android&hl=en_US&gl=US

A great app for recording your dreams.

**Somnio: Dream Journal**
https://play.google.com/store/apps/details?id=com.elixsr.somnio&hl=en_US&gl=US
A great app for recording your dreams.

# ONLINE ARTICLES

https://amerisleep.com/blog/how-to-lucid-dream
An article explaining the benefits of lucid dreaming, offering a range of ways to do it. This is extremely useful when trying different ways to trigger a lucid dream.

https://www.vox.com/platform/amp/science-and-health/2017/7/7/15792188/placebo-effect-explained
This article explains the weird power of the placebo effect. It gives examples of the ways the placebo effect has been proven during real experiments and the positive effects it can have on the brain.

# ACKNOWLEDGMENTS

Without the help of a few people, writing this book would have been incredibly challenging.

I'd love to thank my close friends Julie and Daniel for always being there to support me during the writing process and motivating me to push out the best version of this book possible.

Without the help of Ulysses Press, I would not have had the chance to write this book. Thank you to everybody who worked on the book, and Kierra for introducing me to this opportunity while supporting me with everything I needed in times of doubt and uncertainty.

# ABOUT THE AUTHOR

**Mari Sei** is a young adult who, after growing up in a spiritual family, has an intense interest in all things related to spiritualism. After extensive research, she found a passion in the exploration of reality shifting. Currently studying as a university student, Mari also helps people gain more experience with reality shifting on the side, leading a thriving online community of shifters working together toward a common goal.